HUNTING
An Introductory Handbook

HUNTING
An Introductory Handbook

R. W. F. POOLE

DAVID & CHARLES
Newton Abbot London
North Pomfret (Vt)

Title page
The Quorn Hunt after meeting at Willoughby on the
Wolds in Leicestershire, a popular meet in the
Monday country

To my wife

Line illustrations by Alastair Jackson

British Library Cataloguing in Publication Data
Poole, R. W. F.
    Hunting: an introductory handbook.
    1. Hunting
    I. Title
    799.2

    ISBN 0-7153-9027-9

© Photographs on pp2-3, 10, 24, 33, 47, 50,
62-3, 66, 74, 94, 107, 111, 113, 118, 139,
    153 and 178: Jim Meads 1988
© Photographs on pp19, 39, 69, 81,
98, 122, 128, 131 and 163: Ian Hogg 1988

© Text: R. W. F. Poole 1988

Phototypeset by ABM Typographics Ltd Hull
and printed in Great Britain
by Butler & Tanner Limited, Frome
for David & Charles Publishers plc
Brunel House Newton Abbot Devon

Published in the United States of America
by David & Charles Inc
North Pomfret   Vermont   05053   USA

Contents

1
Hunting as a Way of Life

REASONS FOR HUNTING

Why do people hunt? It is a difficult question to answer for there are probably as many reasons as there are people who hunt, the human animal being a complex creature. The one thing that they should all have in common is that they enjoy it. Hunting is supposed to be fun. If you do not enjoy it, or at any time cease to enjoy it, you would be well advised to give it up at once. Have no regard to principalities and powers; ignore all social, domestic and/or other pressures; if *you* do not get pleasure from it, do not do it. The person who hunts and does not like it, even perhaps hates every minute of it, is a truly unhappy creature and greatly to be pitied. Hunting can involve considerable expense, great physical discomfort and frequent mental disorder; only eventual pleasure, or hope of spiritual salvation, can justify all that.

Most people start hunting because it is part of a way of life they are brought up with; they take it in with their mother's milk. For them there is nothing extraordinary about going hunting. It is as natural as eating or sleeping, and as much a part

of their lives. The only thing they find odd about hunting is that anyone should find it an odd thing to do. The natural hunter is unlikely to analyse his reasons for hunting; psychology is unlikely to be one of his, or her, interests. He is righteously indignant if anyone accuses him of cruelty, and with some justification. He is almost certainly the owner of a large number of domestic animals, all of which he cares for with skill, affection and dedication, albeit without much mawkish sentiment. He may well be a farmer, in which case he will argue pragmatically that cruelty = bad stockmanship = loss of money = bankruptcy. However the natural hunter accepts killing as a perfectly natural thing. If he did not rear sheep for other people to eat, there would be precious few sheep about. He does not believe that the fox enjoys being hunted, but neither does he believe that the fox is unduly worried about it most of the time. He has probably never heard of anthropomorphism, but simply says that experience has taught him that it is nonsense to suggest that animals think like humans. He would probably not go on to say that it is the gift of imagination that lifts humans above brute creation, because he is most unlikely to have come across that sort of thing in any of the books he reads.

The natural hunter probably makes up the large proportion of people who go hunting, but a substantial minority do not belong to this group, and by virtue of the fact that you are reading this book it is more than possible that you do not belong to it either. Why then do you want to hunt?

It is unlikely that your reason is an insatiable blood lust, whatever anyone may say. Very few people who hunt ever see a fox killed, and many of them do not like it when they do. Yet you will see people sitting on their horses apparently well pleased whilst hounds are breaking up their fox, and foot followers, who normally have trouble shuffling down to the Dog and Pullet, will tear through thicket and stream to be present at the obsequies. The reason is that the kill is the logical result of a hunt, it is the orgasm. I apologise if that word offends you, but

remember the urge to hunt is a very ancient and basic one. This book makes no pretence at any psychology, but it does seem probable most ancient and basic urges have some sort of related base; so if it is not blood lust, quite possibly it is some atavistic compulsion.

The thrill of the chase can lie dormant for generations until something, or someone, triggers it off. It is not uncommon for an innocent urban man who has led a hitherto blameless and unexceptionable life, to fall in with a hunt whilst on a gentle rural outing, and to be so intoxicated by the excitement of the whole thing that his life is changed thenceforth. It is only fair to issue a warning here; hunting can become a serious addiction. It may improve your health, but it can have a deleterious effect on marriage, family life and bank balance. Hunting can stimulate the adrenalin to an alarming extent, and there are those who would do better to leave their adrenalin quietly stagnating.

There are those who hunt and yet have little interest in the hunting itself. They hunt for the fresh air and the purposeful exercise. The memory occurs of a man who followed foxhounds on foot wearing a pedometer. He never missed a day, and would walk furiously until his pedometer registered 20 miles, whereupon he would go home regardless of what hounds happened to be doing at the time. For him hunting provided a reason for walking, nothing else, and why not?

Some people hunt because it takes them to hidden corners of the country that they would never see in the normal course of their lives. There is no doubt that hunters enjoy immense privileges of access to parts of the countryside that others do not reach, a fact that causes unhappiness, and envy, amongst groups such as the Ramblers' Association. Hunting has taken me to just such remote and beautiful places, and, whilst the hunting that has taken me there is my main preoccupation, I am not so dull of soul that a combination of autumn colours on the Borders and a view of sixty miles of rolling hills fails to thrill me. I just happen to think that any view is improved if it

The Cottesmore hounds in full cry

contains a pack of hounds in full cry.

Strange as it may sound, there are those who go hunting to frighten themselves. They seek the biggest places to jump, the steepest hills to gallop down. You might think they would be better suited by going eventing, and indeed many of them do that as well. The thing about hunting is that you cannot walk the course beforehand. You do not always know what awaits you on the other side of that stiff black fence; you do not always see the rabbit hole that your horse puts its foot in whilst travelling at 30mph. It is the thrill of the uncertainty that attracts some people; like the man who took a stiffish fence and as he came over the top found himself looking down on a woman on a horse looking up at him, with her mouth open. He

had jumped unknowingly into a sunken lane. An interested spectator said afterwards that as he came over the fence the man said 'Jesus Christ', and by the time he reached the bottom, he had managed the entire Lord's Prayer. Not without effect, it must be said, because the man and his horse missed the woman and her horse, landed together, and galloped off without missing a beat. The drop was afterwards measured at 22 feet. I know, because I was there. I was the man on the horse. It is only fair to add that I had no intention of frightening myself, and I only jumped the fence because the horse was running away with me and there was nothing I could do about it. But there are people who jump those sort of places for the pleasure of the relief when they get safely over them, and who take pleasure in boasting about their falls if they do not.

The category should also include the 'Man who hunts to astonish others', by his feats of derring do. This is probably not a good reason for someone to take up hunting. The category is fairly heavily oversubscribed in a lot of countries, and hunting does not really need any more of them. However, that is a subjective judgement from one whose job it is to pick up the pieces and smooth the feathers that are not infrequently ruffled by the astonishment brigade.

Some people hunt because they like dressing up. There is no doubt that full hunting fig, when properly worn, is very smart. Some are prepared to make a fairly hefty investment for the pleasure of being looked at on the ride out, and the ride home. It seems a harmless little vanity, and a perfectly valid reason for paying a hunt subscription, thereby subsidising rather more active hunters. If you want to hunt for that reason, then go for it, you are not obliged to feel any sense of shame.

It does not really matter what your reason for hunting is, as long as you get pleasure out of it. It may give you instant pleasure, or the pleasure may grow on you; give it a fair trial. If it does not agree with you, for whatever reason, then give it up, for your own sake and that of others.

HISTORY OF HUNTING

Hunting is probably the second oldest human activity. When one of our ape-derived ancestors threw away his apple, swung out of his tree, picked up a stick, brayed something small and furry over the head with it and ate the corpse, he became the first human to hunt. His descendants are still at it today.

The early hunters did it for food. Success in the chase meant the difference between surviving and starving, and the successful hunter became a man of status in his family, clan or tribe. This status still maintains, and skilled hunters are household names, at least in those households where hunting forms a topic for conversation.

As the centuries slipped away, hunting evolved from being a primary source of food procurement, and came to be regarded as having other virtues:

> The practical advantages of hunting are many. It makes the body healthy, improves the sight and the hearing and keeps men from growing old. It affords the best training for war. For men who are sound in mind and body stand always on the threshold of success.

That statement seems as sound today as it doubtless seemed to Xenophon (c400 BC). Soldiers in the better regiments of the British army still regard hunting as an essential part of their training to guard us all against the Asiatic hordes that menace us from the East. There are those who say that the virtues gained in the hunting field will not be much use when we are all incinerated by nuclear fission. They are probably right, but if they went hunting instead of moping about they would be brighter and better human beings, and make a better class of atomic fallout when the time comes. Or, as King Alfred so neatly put it: 'If thou hast a trouble tell it not to a weakling, but to thy saddle bow and ride singing forth.'

The Celts were great hunters, and hounds from Britain were

much sought after by the Romans. The Saxons, too, seem to have been fond of hunting, and the aforementioned Alfred was renowned as 'a most expert and active hunter'. They appear to have been a rather jolly people. The Saxon kings introduced the Forest system. This is not to say that they started planting trees everywhere; in this context 'forest' merely meant an area set aside as a royal hunting preserve. No man might 'meddle with the King's Game', but apart from that all men were free to hunt on their own ground. The Saxons were also responsible for bringing in a close season, known as the 'fence months', when hunting was not permitted. November then as now was the start of the season proper. The Anglo Saxon name for November was *blot monath*, the 'blood month'.

The free and easy ways of the Saxons came to an abrupt halt after the Norman Conquest. The Norman kings were all fond of hunting, but they were jolly well not going to let anyone else in on the fun. Great areas of England were afforested, that is became royal preserves. Sometimes the native inhabitants were booted out altogether. Even where they were allowed to remain, life was far from comfortable. Common law did not apply in the forests; forest law was the order and it overrode many ancient rights and privileges of farmer and freeholder.

Woe betide the man who tampered with the vert, ie any growing plant big enough to shelter a deer; he would be guilty of assart and, whilst he lived, would wish that he had not. Anyone caught taking venison, which at that time meant any flesh, could be blinded. Good King Richard, he of the Lion Heart and the dubious sexual proclivities, added castration for good measure. For killing a female deer you were liable to be terminated with extreme prejudice.

It is hardly surprising that the native English resented this savage interference with their rights and freedoms. The mounted huntsman became the usurper and the oppressor, and this image became bitterly ingrained in the peasant psyche. We see the legacy of this today, when hunting is represented as part of the class war, with protesters who are not so much interested

in protecting the hunted as in laying one on the hunters.

As the Middle Ages progressed, society became more complicated and more sophisticated, with elaborate rules of ceremony and behaviour governing all aspects of life. Hunting became more formal and scientific under the Code of Venery. Firm rules were laid down as to what was hunted, how, and when. Animals were classified. The beasts for hunting were the hare, hart, wolf and boar. The other category was beasts of the chase. These were subdivided into 'beasts of sweet flight' and 'beasts of stinking flight'. 'Sweet flight' included buck, doe, bear, reindeer and elk. The 'stinkers' were such animals as the foulmart, polecat, wild cat, badger, fox, weasel, marten, squirrel, otter, stoat and, believe it or not, the white rat.

The late Middle Ages, and the Tudor era, brought great physical and social change to England. The old feudal society was in decline, with a corresponding rise in the importance of the yeoman and the gentry. The royal forests declined in area and importance. It must be remembered that during the Middle Ages much of England was still covered in woodland. As the population increased, more land was cleared for agriculture. There was also a greatly increased demand for timber for the navy and for industry. The result of all this was that not only did many of the 'beasts' disappear along with their habitat (the last wolf in England was killed during the reign of Elizabeth I), but there arose an independent class of squires and country gentlemen who were able to indulge their inbred passion for hunting, as did the great lords. But they had to find something to hunt.

The hart (red deer), and the buck (fallow) were still extant, but increasingly they were confined to the deer parks of the great estates, whilst the wild deer were being pushed back, by creeping civilisation, into the wilder corners of the country. There does not seem to be any record of a serious attempt to hunt roe with hounds in this country, during the last three hundred years. This is strange as roe deer hunting is popular in France. It is possible that they were not numerous enough in

the past to provide regular sport. Their numbers have certainly exploded in England during the last thirty years.

The hare was still the favoured quarry. Harehunting was regarded as being 'full of subtlety and craft, and possessed of divers delights and varieties which other chases do not afford'. Modern harehunters would heartily endorse this statement, and for pure venery you can do no better than to hunt with a good pack of hare hounds. However, then, as now, there were those who required a little more harooch in their sport, and to supply this fascinating ingredient these sportsmen turned to the fox.

The fox had always been hunted, but only as vermin to be harried, bullied, and killed by all means possible. The medieval hunting chroniclers of the chase, such as Twici and Markham, were scathing about the fox as a quarry. Everyman's hand was against him, and it was some time before he achieved the position of honour that he holds in most hunting countries today. Incidentally, in hunting circles a fox, unless known to be a vixen, is always masculine; hares, on the other hand, are always referred to as 'she'.

The first record of a purpose bred pack of foxhounds appears to be in a book written by Sir Thomas Cockaine, a Derbyshire squire, during the reign of the first Elizabeth. But whilst Sir Thomas certainly kept and hunted foxhounds, he appears to have hunted other quarry as well.

It seems certain that foxhunting was establishing itself as a regular and respectable sport throughout the seventeenth century. One of the best known of the early foxhunters was the 2nd Duke of Buckingham. He seems to have kept hounds in Buckinghamshire for a time, but when he disgraced himself at Court he retired to his Yorkshire estates. From Helmsley Castle he hunted a large area round Bilsdale, Farndale and Ryedale. He is reputed to have shown great sport, and to have been a highly popular master of hounds. It is possible that he was also the first man to beggar himself through foxhunting. He caught a chill whilst digging out a fox on the moors, and is supposed to have died in the 'worst room, in the worst inn, in

Kirkby Moorside'. The hounds continued, and eventually became the Sinnington Hunt, which continues to this day and has justice in its claim to be the oldest pack of foxhounds in England.

It was during the eighteenth century that foxhunting could be said to have become a national pastime. Many local squires and yeomen maintained their own local packs of harriers, hunting on their own and their neighbours' land, but the foxhound packs were becoming rather grand affairs run by great landowners, and hunting over vast tracts of land. For instance Lord Berkeley's hounds hunted from Bristol to Wormwood Scrubs. Four separate kennels were maintained to hunt this vast country, and hounds would progress from one to another. One of the kennels was at Charing Cross, and hounds used to hunt round Gray's Inn Fields and Islington.

It was in 1762 that the 5th Duke of Beaufort, after an abortive day's deer hunting, found a fox in Silk Wood and had such a good hunt that thereafter he turned to hunting the fox entirely. He also hunted a vast country from north of Bristol to Banbury in Oxfordshire.

It is worth remembering that although the areas were vast, the country was very different to the sort of countryside that we know today. The rural vista of copse and hedgerow has been almost entirely man made during the last two hundred years. In the eighteenth century the country would have been much more open, with vast areas of common land and many fewer enclosures. Apart from the relics of the great forests, coverts would have been few and far between; the purpose-grown fox and game coverts, which is what most of our small woodlands are, were yet to come. Because of the openness of the country, and the lack of any tradition of fox preserving at that time, foxes would have been scarce by modern standards. All this changed as more and more landowners took an interest in sport and the improvement of agriculture. The Enclosure Acts were put through Parliament, allowing landowners to enclose and fence common land for their own benefit and with

'If it wasn't for those damned hounds!'

often scant regard for the rights of the Commoners: 'The law will punish man or woman, who steal a goose from off the Common. But lets the greater felon loose, who steals the Common from the goose.'

In 1752 Hugo Meynell bought the hounds of Thomas Boothby, in Leicestershire, and took over his country, comprising what is now the Quorn and the Fernie countries. Hugo Meynell is usually regarded as the father of modern foxhunting, both as a breeder of what became the basis of the modern foxhound, and as the founder of the scientific approach to hunting. By the time Meynell retired, in 1800, Leicestershire was firmly established as the fashionable centre of foxhunting, and hunting in its modern form could be said to have started.

In the nineteenth century, foxhunting became fashionable. The ride became as important as the hunt, indeed more so in the fashionable countries. There is the story of the Leicestershire 'blood' larking across country on the way home from hunting, and shouting out to a friend, 'what fun we would have out hunting, if it was not for those damned hounds'; some of his ilk are still to be found today. A wise man once said that the

interest of the followers of a hunt in their hounds was in inverse proportion to the excellence of their country for riding over; but more of that anon.

To become a MFH in Victorian England was to become a great man, on a social par with the Lord Lieutenant. Most masters would have been drawn from the gentry and the aristocracy, and increasingly from the plutocracy. It was necessary to be rich. Many of the family packs were private, taking no subscriptions and selecting their followers. Even the subscription packs provided only a small proportion towards the total expenditure of running a hunt. The master was expected to pay, and pay handsomely, for the privilege of mastership.

One of the strengths of hunting is that it has always attracted a number of people of high intelligence, and over the last two hundred years very clever and able enthusiasts have given a great deal of thought to the science of hunting and to the breeding of the right sort of hound to put that science into practice. Victorian foxhunters had time and money to carry out such theories, and to establish a basis for the craft of hunting which maintains to this day. The nineteenth century produced the two great textbooks on hunting; these are Peter Beckford's *Thoughts on Hunting*, and Thomas 'Craven' Smith's *Diary of a Huntsman*.

There are those who describe the period 1870–1914 as the Golden Age of hunting. The farming depression of the 1870s put most of England back to grass, wire had hardly begun to make itself felt. There had been some apprehension about the spread of the railways; but instead of making hunting impossible, as some faint hearts had feared, the railway system had actually made hunting more accessible to those who lived in towns. A horse box could be attached to an express train on demand, and mount and rider whisked in unheard of speed and comfort from almost anywhere to just about everywhere. The Percy Hunt (Northumberland) pre-1914 ran a hunt train from the station beside the kennels to hunt the north end of the country. The train would wait in the siding to bring them home

The West Percy fell X hounds

again. Total hire charge was £3 per day. This was the high period of Victorian prosperity, and much of that prosperity was directed into matters sporting.

Many people thought that World War I would mean the end of hunting, but hunting continued throughout the war; albeit with vastly depleted kennels, studs and staffs. As Lord Lonsdale said at the time, there had to be something for people to look forward to when they came home on leave.

Hunting continued in great style throughout the twenties and thirties. This was a period that produced not only some of the greatest huntsmen of the century, but also some great hound breeders and hunting intellectuals. World War II failed to stop hunting, but in post-war Britain socialist controls and swingeing taxes made things more difficult for everybody, and for the first time there was a challenge to hunting in Parliament. The legacies of the Norman forest laws and the Enclosure Acts

were coming home to roost.

I first became addicted to hunting in the 1950s. At that time hunting seemed to be sinking into a coma. Few people hunted, and they tended to be middle aged and elderly. The whole affair has changed dramatically during the last thirty years. On the whole, people have become richer, more mobile, and have more spare time. There are more horses about now than there have been since 1914. There has been a tremendous upsurge of interest in all field sports, with more people wanting to hunt, shoot and fish than ever before. This increase of enthusiasm has not been without its problems. Britain has undergone an agricultural revolution in the last fifteen years. Farming has become more intensive, and expensive, and farmers have become correspondingly more sensitive about access to their land. Every year more land disappears under roads and houses; our countryside shrinks all the time. At the same time there has been greatly increased pressure from urban man, not only for access to the countryside but for the countryside to be changed to something more approaching his rural idyll.

Hunting is not part of urban man's rural idyll. He knows nothing about it, but is convinced that it must be a bloodthirsty anachronism because his daily popular newspaper has told him that it is. It is easy to see how strange hunting must seem to the gentle inhabitants of Penge or Beckenham. They never see death, apart from the odd bit of battered fur on the main road that may once have been a cat. Any trace of the old wild urge to hunt has been bred out, or sublimated into some sterile urban activity. Rural man accepts death as the inevitable end to all life. He is still close enough to nature to regard killing as a natural function; it happens in the wildlife all around him all the time. It is also perfectly natural to him to wring a chicken's neck, or to hunt a fox, and he is bewildered by and resentful of urban man's attempts to interfere with this way of life.

Hunting in the 1980s is in a strange position. It is attracting more support, over a wider social spectrum, than it ever has. It is also under greater threat than ever before. Now that it has

been dragged into the political arena, it would be naïve to think that its enemies will be willing to see it leave in any other way except flat on its back on a stretcher. Time alone will tell.

HUNTING AS A SOCIAL FORCE

In many rural areas, especially the more remote ones, the local hunt is a focal point of social activity. Most hunts operate a supporters' club. This has two functions, social and financial. Many clubs make a large contribution to hunt funds and assist in such things as the purchase of vehicles, or even horses, and in the maintenance of the kennels. To raise this finance the clubs run endless fund raising functions – dances, whist drives, bring and buy, cheese and wine parties, hunter trials, team chases, darts leagues, sheep dog trials, horse shows etc – the list is apparently endless. To be an active member of an active hunt supporters' club is to be very active indeed; you may have some dull moments, but you will seldom be allowed to have an idle one.

As you would expect, these club functions are supported by hunt members, but they also provide jollification for non hunting people in the surrounding area. Thus there is a continuous goodwill and public relations element to these activities. *In vino veritas* applies, and many niggles that might otherwise fester, tumefy and are then soothed.

This not the whole social scene. There is the Hunt Ball. This usually has its own organising committee, and may be regarded as a social highlight. The great coup is for the organisers to persuade the owner of some stately home to host the frolic. Owners of stately homes, however, tend to be wary of accepting such an honour, for hunting people tend to take seriously the business of enjoying themselves. Some 350 hunters enjoying themselves seriously is not a thing to be considered lightly, and problems do arise, of which Ming vases full of vomit, and misuse of the stately owner's bed, are but two of the lesser ones. There was a report of a stately home where they moved all the

The point-to-point

furniture upstairs, sealed the stairs with barbed wire, and stationed the head keeper with a shotgun and a bottle of whisky behind it; but it may have been an exaggeration. For the socially inclined hunter the Hunt Ball is not to be missed, and tickets tend to get snapped up early. You are welcome to mine, I hate the wretched things.

Most hunts have a point-to-point. This is again a money spinner, and a social occasion where town meets country. Quite a few anti-hunting people go to point-to-points, because they do not twig that they are linked to hunts. If you enjoy watching bad racing and eating soggy picnics on a windswept steppe, then point-to-points are a must for you, as they are for thousands of others. You will undoubtedly meet lots of nice people, even if you never see a horse. But you will not see me.

From all this you will perceive that the hunt looms large in the lives of people in country districts, even if they are not active partakers in the sport themselves. By the same token the state of the local hunt is a matter for comment and concern in shops, pubs and drawing rooms, and rightly so, because it affects the morale of an entire area.

Everybody likes to see a well-conducted hunt with a respected mastership. When morale is high in a hunt country, with hounds hunting well and catching foxes, and when there is mutual confidence between those who hunt and those whose land is hunted over, the whole area benefits. Nothing succeeds like success, and people like success about them, even if they are not directly involved.

The converse is also true. A dismal hunt where there is disagreement and bickering is an unhappy affair. Hunting provokes strong feelings, and there are no worse rows than an internecine hunt row, which can poison relationships over a whole district. It has to be said that there are certain hunts where feuding is endemic. Unless you enjoy that sort of thing and, sadly, there are those who do, I would strongly recommend that you avoid such countries if you can.

HUNTING AS A RURAL INDUSTRY

We have considered hunting as a social force, but what about its economic force, namely hunting as a rural industry? In the hunting season 1985–6 there were 433 packs of hounds in Great Britain and Eire. They were divided up as follows: foxhounds 237, harriers 51, staghounds 6, beagles 110, bassets 12, mink and coypu hounds 17.

Two recent surveys make thoughtful reading. The first was concerned with those packs with mounted followers, that is foxhounds, staghounds and harriers. The report showed that 48,000 people were full hunt subscribers, and that 390,000 others hunted regularly, either mounted or on foot. About 1,000,000 people attended at least one hunt meet per season. Hunting provided direct full-time employment for 13,032 people, and indirect employment for 26,810. Some 48,000 horses were kept to go hunting, so that 9,900 suppliers such as farriers, vets, saddlers, tailors and feed merchants, relied on hunting for part of their income.

The other survey was a government survey on rural employ-

ment. The people conducting the enquiry did an in-depth investigation into the affairs of one hunt which, I understand, was the VWH (Vale of the White Horse) who hunt in Wiltshire and Gloucestershire. The committee found that the VWH had 160 mounted subscribers, and 300 regular car and foot followers. The direct annual expenditure generated by the hunt was £710,000. You can do your own calculations based on those figures, and whichever way you cut it, you will see that hunting is a multi-million pound industry, and nearly all that money is spent in rural areas: food for thought, indeed.

HUNTING AND POLITICS

They are out to get us. That is the unmistakable message that has to be taken on board by all hunt supporters today. So, who are 'they'? They are an interesting melange, ranging from little old ladies who have a genuine horror of killing things but who do not give too much thought to what the meat with which they feed their moggies might once have been, to animal rights activists who have little interest in animal rights but a lot of interest in bringing about social change through violence. Duffing up elderly hunt supporters and breaking into factory farms in the name of animal rights, gets them sympathy from uncomprehending urban masses, and provides useful training for . . ., well for something nasty.

In between, there is a varied, and somewhat motley collection of points of view. There are undoubtedly many people who are sincerely opposed to hunting on moral grounds. Those of us who hunt may feel that their point of view is based on lack of knowledge and misplaced sentiment, but it is, none the less, a genuine and deeply held point of view and must be respected. Then we have the class warriors. They do not actually care very much about animals, but they do care about hunting. To them hunting epitomises a way of life that they hate and want to destroy: hunting is High Toryism, wicked squires and down-trodden peasants. To them a red-faced man

Viewing a fox away from a covert in Grafton country in Northamptonshire with a top hat, red coat and shiny horse offers a fairly useful hate target. They are deeply disappointed if they discover him to be a wages clerk from Pinner who votes something else; never mind, he can be a class traitor instead. And behind the activists is the tabloid press, to whom hunting is manna from whatever a tabloid journalists regards as heaven. All hunts are 'exclusive', all hunters 'red-faced, old Etonian, cavalry officers', hunting 'barbaric' – all good, cliché ridden copy.

Last we come to the huddled city dwellers. To them hunting, and the way of life that it is a part of, is as foreign as the life of the Amazonian Indians. And because it is different and little understood, they vaguely feel it must be wrong. In the same way they vaguely feel that rural England is wrong, and should be stopped. England would be a better and happier place if it was all New Towns with nice little bits of park in between, where the kiddies and the dog could be exercised. As for the country dwellers, well they are only 4 per cent of the population, let them go the way of all minority groups; consign them to oblivion and let them take their nasty, anachronistic sports with them.

The facts of life are that during the last hundred years, England has been transformed from an agrarian to an urban society, and the years since World War II have seen immense social changes. Political power has shifted away from the great landowners and knights of the shires, and has gone into the hands of the urban middle classes. These new elected representatives have little interest in rural matters beyond having a weekend cottage. Their environment and conditioning is unlikely to make them sympathetic to hunting, and as career politicians, of whatever persuasion, their first approach to any matter is 'what votes are there in it for me?' Unless a politician represents some particularly cohesive rural constituency, he will probably consider that he will win more votes, and avoid conflict with the more strident special interest groups, by opposing hunting.

If hunting is to survive it has to become as good or better

than its opponents at political activism. At the time of writing, hunting people still seem to bask in a sort of bucolic complacency. 'They'll never stop hunting', is something that one hears oft repeated. I fear that it is a form of whistling in the dark. If we do not bestir ourselves, they will.

2
How Hunting is Organised

PRIVATE AND SUBSCRIPTION PACKS

The running and maintaining of a pack of hounds has never been a cheap undertaking, and the bottom line is always who finally pays the bills. In the early days of hunting there was no doubt at all about how it was done. If you kept a pack of hounds for your own amusement, you paid for their maintenance and did what you liked about hunting, just as you did whatever you liked with the rest of your estate. This was the top end of the scale.

The other end was the trencher-fed pack. A few local enthusiasts would band together for the purpose of hunting; they would maintain no kennel and keep no staff or, at most, a part-time huntsman. Each member would keep a hound at home at his own expense. On hunting days, either the 'walker' would bring his hound to the place of meeting, or the huntsman would go round collecting each one in the morning. Hounds always know when it is a hunting day, and it seems that trencher-fed hounds were no exception. They would often be waiting for the huntsman at some convenient lane end or

crossroads. At the end of the hunting day, the hounds would simply peel off and make their own way to their individual homes. This was obviously a very cost effective, if not terribly efficient, way of running a hunt. It was a method that tended to produce a collection of individuals rather than a pack of hounds – a technical distinction, perhaps, but an important one. Quite naturally all the hound walkers would want a say in the running of the hunt, and would not be backward either in helping the huntsman to hunt the hounds. You should read the works of R. S. Surtees for descriptions of such packs. They were called 'trencher fed' because each hound went home to his individual trencher, or dish, instead of being fed at the communal trough as he would be in an orthodox kennel.

Although rarer than they were in Surtees's day, trencher-fed packs still exist, notably in the remoter parts of Ireland, with probably no less than five trencher-fed packs based in Cork City. Most of the English Lakeland packs are semi trencher fed, being kennelled during the hunting season but dispersed to farms during the summer.

To return to the private packs; in the course of the nineteenth century there was a mushrooming of their numbers. There was not always a local magnate, rich or willing enough to take on the hounds, so the local landowners would form a committee of management and would guarantee a certain sum of money to someone who was prepared to take on the mastership. The guarantee was raised by an annual subscription and the master was responsible for all the expenses of hunting the country, of which the guarantee, as we saw in the previous chapter, would seldom cover more than a small percentage. Thus the subscription pack came into being.

The master appointed to head a subscription pack was not necessarily a local man. There were people who were keen enough, and rich (or cunning) enough, to take a country removed from the one in which they were bred and buttered. Indeed there was often competition to take on one of the better countries, a situation that still maintains to the present day. A

'bagman' master was still required to be rich, his financial commitment was open-ended, and people who hunt have never liked having to pay for their sport; that situation also maintains to the present day.

One thing that has changed is the situation regarding the hounds. At one time they would have been the sole property of the master. On taking on the mastership of a country, a man would have to buy his hounds. Often he would do a deal with his predecessor to take over the existing pack, it being the custom to throw in the feed trough, and a terrier, free. At one time, if a hunting man developed a reputation for parsimony he was referred to as 'the sort of chap who would charge you for the trough'. The other option was to buy draft hounds from another pack. These are quite simply hounds that are surplus to requirements in their home kennels, and who are put on the transfer list. These days hounds are seldom sold, and then only to recognised packs. If you a civilian, as it were, wanted to go and buy a foxhound to impress the chaps at the golf club it would be theoretically impossible for you to obtain one, which is fortunate for both you and the foxhound. Draft hounds can be a somewhat doubtful quantity, because nobody gets rid of his good animals. It is considered extremely bad form to give away a bad hound, but human nature being what it is, stranger things have been known to happen.

In the old days, besides the option of applying to a chosen kennel for the privilege of buying their drafts, it was possible to go to Messrs Tattersall's hound sales at Rugby and bid for what was wanted. It was unlikely that you would have been able to buy a fairy queen for fourpence. Hounds were not cheap. A price of several hundred guineas for a couple was not uncommon for hounds with sought after blood lines. The Rugby sales continued certainly until World War I, and possibly into the twenties.

Once our master had collected his hounds, they were then his property, yea, they and their issue from generation to generation. Some packs are still privately owned, but the general

A good hound

rule, these days, is for the hounds to belong to the country. Whilst the master is normally responsible for their breeding, and will refer to them as 'his' hounds, legally they are not, and if he were to up sticks and off with them, the hunt committee would have every right to set the peelers on to him. However if a master gives a hound to another master, that hound after joining the pack is regarded as his own personal property, but its get will belong to the hunt.

A study of that fascinating reference book, *Baily's Hunting Directory*, shows how the private pack declined faced with the roaring tides of inflation and taxation. Baily's for the season 1897–8 still had many packs that were known by the name of their master and owner, rather than the territorial nomenclature by which they are known today. Most of them carried the telling entry: 'The Master has no guarantee; there is no subscription, and capping is not practised.' In other words, a private pack, carried on at the master's expense, and at his convenience, and just don't you forget it.

The twentieth century has seen a great social evolution, with a massive redistribution of personal wealth. In 1986 there was

only one pack of foxhounds in England that could properly be described as a private pack within the meaning of the act. There are still family packs where the hounds remain the property of one family, who provide hereditary masters, and considerable financial subsidy. But all these packs take subscriptions, thereby giving the subscribers every right to voice their grievances in public, and to receive a polite and sympathetic hearing. That is the theory, but if and when you come to have dealings with some of the masters concerned, you will appreciate how little theory may accord with practice.

HUNTING COUNTRIES

Reference has been made to 'countries', and this requires some elaboration. Every hunt – hare, fox or stag – has its own territory, or country, with strictly defined boundaries. In the early days of hunting there were no such well-defined areas, but as the number of packs increased so did the desire for territorial acquisition. The nineteenth century saw some memorable disputes over who hunted what bit of country, even to the extent of rival packs hunting the same territory. It was obvious that this situation could not be allowed to continue, and that there must be some body to which inter-hunt disputes could be referred for arbitration. Boodles, the gentleman's club in St James's, has a strong membership of landed proprietors. Towards the end of the last century the MFH Committee of Boodles was formed, to which masters brought inter-hunt problems when they could not be solved locally. This committee evolved into the Masters of Foxhounds Association, which is to foxhunting what the Jockey Club is to racing. It advises, cajoles, regulates and, ultimately, disciplines, the conduct of foxhunting in England, Wales and Scotland. The Irish have their own association, which has never recognised partition.

The harehunters, staghunters and minkhunters all have their own associations. Each hunt's area (country) is registered with

The Eryri foxhounds hunting in Snowdonia

the appropriate association; the hunts then have the sole right
to hunt their particular quarry within the defined boundaries
which can only be changed by mutual consent of the hunts
concerned, and under the watchful eye of the masters' association. Whilst boundaries drawn on a map may be effective with
most humans (by no means all), foxes know nothing about
them. The rules are simple. Hunts may pursue a fox into a
neighbour's country and catch it if they can, but they may not
dig it out should it go to ground; neither may they seek another
fox in the neighbour's country having lost, killed or earthed the
hunted one. These rules may be varied by local agreement, or
not, as the case may be. A certain noble MFH often felt
aggrieved by the constant raids into his fair vale by a rough and
ready hill pack. He was properly incensed when it was re-
ported to him that they had run a fox to ground in his country,

and dug the fox out. He wrote a noble four-page tirade to the neighbouring master, and received in reply a single sheet that said simply: 'We allus digs, yr ob servant, N. Spinks.'

The associations have strict written rules of conduct by which their sports are conducted, and which apply to all recognised packs. A 'recognised pack' is simply one that belongs to the association, which the vast majority do or rather their masters, do. No one can be a master of such a pack unless he is a member of the relevant association; only such a pack may hold a point-to-point, and hounds may only be drafted between recognised packs. There are very few unrecognised packs today, but they do exist, mainly in the Celtic twilight of Wales and Cornwall where there is a strong sense of local independence.

OFFICIALS AND STAFF

Each hunting country is a self-perpetuating entity. The hunt committee is composed of local people elected by local people, and usually consists of farmers, landowners and members of the hunt. The committee elects a chairman who should be a man of stature and strong personality. A good chairman should not only be capable of conducting meetings so that the more prolix members are not still rabbiting on in the small hours of the morning, but should also have tact to smooth ruffled feathers and be able to knock heads together when necessary. It is fair to say that too much democracy is not a good thing in a hunting country; too many cooks do indeed make a mess of the broth. The happiest countries are those where there is a strong, respected nob as master or chairman.

There will be a hunt secretary, in most countries an honorary secretary. He or she is responsible for much of the administrative paper work and the collection of hunt funds. The actual scope of the secretary's duties may vary from hunt to hunt, but he is nearly always responsible for raking in the hunt subscriptions and taking the 'cap' (day tickets). If you do not subscribe

'A strong and respected nob as chairman . . .'

to the hunt, you will normally be expected to pay a cap. Some of the bigger hunts have professional, or semi-professional secretaries; their duties are wider, and will include much of the actual administration of the hunting country.

The masters or joint masters are appointed by the committee, who are deemed to represent the country as a whole, although it is often thought politic to ratify appointments through a general meeting of the country. As a rule of thumb, general meetings in a well-run hunt are sparsely attended; a packed general meeting usually equals trouble.

Masters are engaged on an annual basis, their tenure running

from 1 May to 30 April. The MFHA stipulates that all arrangements pertaining to the running of a country must be made by
the first of February, to take effect on the following first of
May. This means that if the committee want to give a master
the elbow, they have to have it all cut and dried by the end of
January.

Most masters are drawn from the local community, and this
is the best way, on the whole, always provided that there is a
local man or woman who has enough knowledge, cash and
local respect to hold down the job. It sometimes happens that,
for a variety of reasons, no local person is either available or
suitable, and then a master must be brought in from outside.

In every generation there are a number of young men who
are ready and willing to devote their lives to hunting; the trick
is to find one who is also solvent, able and available. Good
'professional' masters are a rare, and much sought after, breed.
A hunt may advertise for a master, and indeed may be obliged
to do so by its constitution, and this method may sometimes
deliver the goods. Hunting is a comparatively small world, and
most people involved in it know, or know of, everybody else.
It is fair to say that most hunts are suited by discreet enquiries,
rather than public advertisements.

The Mastership (consisting of one or more masters) has to
come to a financial agreement with the committee for the
running of the country, which boils down to who signs what
cheques. Financial agreements vary from hunt to hunt. The
guarantee system, whereby the hunt guaranteed the masters an
annual sum of money, and the masters were reponsible for the
difference between that amount and the actual annual expenditure, has largely fallen into desuetude. There are still hunts that
are subsidised to a greater or lesser degree by their masters,
but, more and more, people are having to come to terms with
the fact that hunting is expensive, and that if they want to hunt
they are going to have to pay for it.

Once appointed, a master is one of the few remaining
examples of raw power. He is normally responsible for hire,

and fire, of the hunt staff, the breeding of the hounds, the conduct of the hunt kennels and stables, and the management of the country. In most hunts today this is virtually a full-time job for one man.

In a large hunt there will be a staff of up to twenty people to manage. The country will consist of a thousand or more farms, to which the hunt will require access. This means that a thousand farmers and their families must agree to this access, and it is fair to say that whether they do or not will depend to a large degree on their personal relationship with the master. In the course of the season it is inevitable that things will go wrong, and tempers will fray; it is the master's job to sort things out and maintain goodwill. The hunt will not be the only user of the countryside. There will be extensive shooting interests, whose needs and whims have to be taken into account. In many areas a wary eye has to be cocked at local councils and pressure groups, with whom some sort of contact has to be established. It all takes time, tact and endless patience.

Out hunting, the master's power is absolute. I say 'his', but there are many lady masters, who may look like Dresden shepherdesses, but I here tell you that they are not. The master is responsible for the conduct of the day's sport and for the behaviour and good conduct of all those comprising what is loosely referred to as the hunt, even though most of the followers are in the grip of various types of strong emotion. With all this in mind, you will appreciate that masters tend to be strongish characters; they are permitted a certain amount of colourful behaviour and freedom of expression in the interests of maintaining good order and discipline. If your conduct falls below the required standard, the master is perfectly entitled to bring this fact to your attention. It is best if he does this quietly and politely, but if you transgress at a moment of heat, when several things are happening very quickly, you are quite likely to get an old-fashioned bollocking. You may not like this, no one does much; but then it is not much fun to have to sort out the mess that your crime may have caused; you will just have to

debit enjoyment and credit experience. It is considered normal practice to raise your hat to the master at the meet and to wish him 'Good morning'. You should address him as 'Master', until that heady moment when he invites you to call him Ron or Peregrine.

If you feel unable to accept his discipline, the master is perfectly within his rights to send you home and, in extreme cases of uncivil disobedience, to take the hounds home and leave the full weight of public opinion to bear upon your shoulders. In my experience masters seldom use these ultimate deterrents. I have only once seen hounds taken home, and that after gross misconduct by a portion of the field; I have only twice sent a person home. It is the big stick, to be used with caution, and masters tend to exert control by force of personality; but you have been warned.

One of the masters, or someone appointed by them, will be in charge of the field – the field master. You read of people 'taking their own line across country'; this is no longer possible in most countries. It is the master's duty to conduct the field across the country so as to give them the maximum possible fun, subject to the conditions laid upon him by the local landowners. For instance, on Farm A it may be a case of spread out, kick on and help yourselves. This may not be the case on neighbouring Farm B, where access is only allowed along agreed, and strictly controlled, routes. You do not know this, and if you go barging on regardless you may well get the hunt warned off Farm B altogether. So I beg of you, do listen to what you are told, and do as you are asked to do.

Some masters hunt their own hounds; some employ a professional huntsman. Hunt service is a risky profession that continues to attract young men of very high calibre. The pay is poor, the hours limitless, and the work hard and often dirty. Yet there is excitement and glamour too. It is not a job, but a way of life that many young men fall in love with. Professional hunt servants tend to be men of very high calibre. They should be treated with courtesy and respect. They are persons of great

The whipper-in watching a ride

honour in the countryside, and because they have old-fashioned manners and call you Sir or Madam, this does not mean that you may patronise or abuse them. They are the personal servants of the master.

The traditional way for a young man to start in hunt service was as a strapper in the stables, doing two or three horses. He would then progress to second horseman. He would still be working in the stables, but on hunting days he would take out the second horse for one of the hunt staff, and return home with the first one. His next step would have been a second whipper-in's post. He would now be working in the kennel under the often terrifying eye of the huntsman. In time he would progress to be first whipper-in. The past tense is relevant because increased costs have forced reductions in the num-

The huntsman

bers of men employed in recent years in most hunts; the result is that men take short cuts in their careers that are often of benefit neither to them, nor the sport.

The whipper-in is the huntsman's assistant, and even today there may be more than one. He has two main functions. The first is to see that the huntsman has all his hounds all the time; ie should the hounds divide during a hunt, it is the whipper-in's job to stop those who are deemed to be in error and reunite them with the main pack. His other main duty is to prevent

trouble before it happens. If hounds are going along a road and a foxy looking ginger tom whisks across their track, a good whipper-in will be on the spot whilst the hounds are still scratching their heads and wondering whether it is a fox or not. If hounds are running hard towards a main road and danger, the whipper-in should be there before them.

The huntsman, or kennel huntsman, is the top of the tree. A kennel huntsman whips in to a master who hunts his own hounds; but he enjoys the same status as the professional huntsman, and if he does not always enjoy the same excitements, neither is he subject to quite the same pressures.

The bigger hunts will have the staff ride two horses during the day. A hunt horse does much more work than yours will do, and a change of horse saves wear and tear. The second horses are ridden by the second horsemen, would you believe!

Most hunts have a terrier man, either amateur or professional. He is usually to be located in a battered Land Rover stuffed with terriers, spades and gnarled men in old overcoats. You may have reservations about the use of terriers out hunting, but there are countries where hunting would be impossible without them. For many people, a dig is the main part of the day's sport. If you attend a dig it is best not to get in the way, or make a nuisance of yourself. Terrier men tend to be robust characters, and proud of their craft. I once had to rescue a man who was being chased across a field by an infuriated, spade-wielding terrier man. The offender had offered one bit of gratuitous advice too many.

There is no doubt that hunting a pack of hounds is one of the most exciting and challenging things that a man can do. It is fascinating, frustrating and totally absorbing. It is also extremely difficult to do well. Well done, it gives an immense amount of pleasure to a great many people. Good huntsmen, amateur or professional, hold a position of honour in country life, and that is no bad thing for any man to aspire to.

3
How to Start

If you wish to take up hunting, you will have to narrow your choice. You will have to decide what sort of hunting you want to start off with. In Britain you may choose between hunting fox, fallow buck, red deer, hare and mink (summer only). You have the alternatives of hunting on a horse, on foot, in a car, on a bicycle, or various permutations of them all. Your choice will be affected by various factors such as where you live, how much you want to spend on your sport, and what you want to get out of it. Let us consider the options that may be open to you.

There are very few parts of England that are not within fairly easy reach of a pack of foxhounds, and it should not present any great difficulty for anyone to find out where their nearest pack is. It does not matter if it is not a very good one; if you are a beginner you are not going to know the difference anyway, your critical faculties will increase with experience.

The situation is similar for harehunters. Beagle packs are well spread about the country, and there is bound to be one within easy reach of where you live. Mounted harehunting

(harriers) is not quite so easy to find. Most of the harrier packs are either in East Anglia, Lancashire or the West Country, where most of them hunt fox anyway, just to simplify matters! The fallow buck is only hunted in the New Forest. The red deer is hunted by three packs in north Devon and Somerset, and nowhere else. If you want any form of hunting in summer, mink hunting is all that is available. It is pedestrian, pleasant, and semi aquatic; there are many worse things that you could be doing on a fine summer's day.

MOUNTED HUNTING

Foxhunting

Foxhunting is the pursuit of the wild red fox with a pack of foxhounds. The fox is the only person involved who knows where he is going, and the hounds hunt him by his scent. Scent is a complicated problem which will be dealt with later in more detail. The efficiency of packs of hounds varies greatly. An efficient pack will probably catch one fox for every five that they hunt. This book is not about the ethics of hunting, but it is probably fair to make the following points. There is no natural predator that preys on the British fox. With hunting, the weakest are killed, and the fittest survive, which is the way of nature. Hunting does not seek to wipe out the fox population, merely to control it. It is quite possible that you will never see hounds kill a fox; many people hunt all their lives without actually seeing a kill. If you do see one, you will appreciate what a quick end it is. If you could slow the tape down, you would see the first hound go for the backbone, to snap the spinal cord. The fox is certainly torn to pieces, or should be by a good pack of hounds, but not alive; by then he is as dead as the bit of steak that you ate the night before with such relish.

Foxhunting should be exciting; there should be an element of haroosh and a spicing of danger. If you are not nervous before a day's foxhunting, there is some essential ingredient lacking in either yourself or your local hunt. Part of the excitement

of hunting the fox is that you never know what is going to happen next; it is what hunting people refer to as 'the glorious uncertainty'. There is an element of formal pageantry about
foxhunting that appeals to a lot of people, and a lot of related
social activity, which many people enjoy. It is safe to say that
90 per cent of the people who hunt on a horse, regard hunting
as another equine activity; they hunt to ride. For the other 10
per cent the horse is merely the most convenient way of following hounds; they ride to hunt. If you want to hunt for the ride,
foxhunting is for you. However if the hounds and the hunting
are your primary interest, you must remember that as a
member of the mounted field you will, with the majority of
packs, see precious little of the hounds as a general rule. The
constraints of modern farming mean that 'taking your own line
across country' has become a thing of the past with most hunts.
You will be 'encouraged' to follow the field master who will
take his flock across country in such a way as to minimise the
pressures on your farming hosts; your wild career may bear
little, or no, relation to where the hounds have actually gone.
In practice you will find that riding with the average provincial
pack will mean riding, in single file, round endless fields of
winter corn and queuing for hunt jumps; you may not see
hounds for an hour at a time. You may think that there is not
much fun in this, and I would agree with you; I would not
enjoy it, but then I have never had to do it. You must make up
your own mind; after all, there must be pleasure in it otherwise
there would not be so many people wanting to take part. Of
course there are countries where you can hunt and have a good
ride, and watch the hounds. They tend to be in the remoter
parts of the realm, and if you have access to such hunting, you
are fortunate, and should appreciate just how lucky you are.
For real hound and fox enthusiasts, the hill countries of the
West, Wales and the Scottish Borders will provide the wild
sport that you cannot but enjoy. However, the very remote-
ness that is part of their charm, means that they are out of most
peoples' reach on a regular basis.

The other thing that has to be said about mounted hunting is that it is expensive; everything to do with horses is expensive. Do not delude yourself that you can do it cheaply. With horses cheap usually means nasty, and you do not want to have anything to do with nastiness. The only way to keep a horse cheaply is to buy a big hill farm and keep a 'shepherding pony' on which you may occasionally, purely by chance you understand, just happen to fall in with the hounds when you are out about the hill; a shepherding pony is tax deductible.

A lot of keen foxhunters follow by car, bicycle or even foot. Many people get a great deal of pleasure from these methods of hunting. Many regular foot followers are much more knowledgeable about hounds and hunting than the mounted followers, and often see more of the actual chase. You can have a great deal of fun hunting in a car, and there has to be a certain satisfaction as you sit in your car warm, dry and chewing a butty, whilst you watch the mounted followers soaking and shivering on that windswept hillside.

Harriers

It may be that you live in an area that boasts a pack of harriers. A harrier is merely another type of hound that is usually used for harehunting, and followed on a horse. I confess that I have never hunted with harriers, but I have always had the impression that it is a rather more sedate sport than foxhunting. For one thing, the hare tends to run in a circle. You are less likely to run as far, or as fast, as you might with foxhounds, and therefore less likely to get lost, which can be a very frustrating experience. All in all, it is possible that going out with the harriers would be a very good way to start mounted hunting, but the opportunity is less available than for foxhunting. There are quite a number of harrier packs in Devon, but they use a different type of hound to the standard harrier – the West Country harrier – and, as already mentioned, they mostly tend to hunt fox exclusively these days.

Staghunting

It would be wrong to leave mounted hunting without touching on staghunting, though this is more fully discussed in Chapter 11. If you get the chance to do it, you should not miss it. It is totally different to foxhunting, but just as fascinating in its own way. I do suggest, however, that it is not suitable for the inexperienced rider, for it can be physically pretty gruelling. A red deer will cover many miles, over wild country, and if you are not up to that sort of riding you will quite simply not enjoy yourself. Perhaps it should be regarded as A-level hunting. People have said to me that they like foxhunting, but do not approve of staghunting; almost invariably it turns out that they have never done it. You have to sample it to understand it, and to understand what an important part of the way of life of the people of north Devon staghunting is. Unfortunately, unless you live in the area, staghunting is hardly a practical proposition.

Foot hunting

Let us now turn to hunting done solely on foot. The first thing to be said is that it is obviously much cheaper than hunting on a horse. Some expenditure is necessary, however. Hunting takes place in all sorts of winds and weather. We will deal with clothing and equipment in more detail later; for the nonce, suffice it to say that for all hunting your aim should be warmth and comfort. To achieve these admirable ends, the foot hunter needs to invest wisely in three main items: a good pair of boots, a warm coat, and a good stick.

Certain parts of Britain are mountainous and unrideable. In these places, mainly Wales and the Lake District, foxhunting is entirely pedestrian. Do not be deceived into thinking that it is easy; you need to be very fit indeed. You will see a bent, hirpling old man set off up a fell at a snail's pace, and you will say to yourself that, if that old crock can get up the hill, then surely you, the pride of the Hogs Norton Lawn Tennis Association, will have no problems; Heaven preserve your inno-

Hunting on foot with the David Davies foxhounds in mid-Wales. They hunt on foot two days a week, and on horses on Saturdays

cence. That old man has been a hill shepherd all his life; he has legs of steel and lungs of leather; he can keep up that pace, up hill, down hill, for hours at a time without tiring; he will leave you bent and gasping within ten minutes. Fell hunting is tremendous fun, and is worth getting yourself a bit fit for. The scenery is glorious but, like all scenery, not so glorious that it is not improved by the inclusion of a pack of hounds.

To most people foot hunting means beagling. The beagle is a jolly little hound that is designed for hunting hares, not for tugging fat ladies down the Promenade at Cheltenham. Beagles are always followed on foot, and beagling is a very good way to get into hunting. Beaglers tend to be a jolly and informal lot of people, prone to excessive facial hair and beer drinking. As the hare tends to run in a circle, you can either be frightfully

The bassethound

energetic and run after the hounds around the outside of the
circle, or you can follow the old and bold to some central vantage point where you can all light your pipes, lean on your
sticks, and watch the hunt happening around you. Whichever
way you do it, you will have a pleasant afternoon amongst
good company, and see a lot of hunting. Harehunting has the
advantage of taking place mostly in the open, whereas

foxhounds can disappear into sylvan fastnesses for whole days at a time. The hare is a fascinating and difficult animal to hunt, and you will see more pure hunting with a good pack of beagles than almost anywhere else.

Bassets have not been mentioned. A basset is a sort of long wheel base beagle, but slower and heavier, with the most marvellous voice. Hunting with them is more fun than hunting with beagles, but that is a personal choice. There are, comparatively, many more packs of beagles than there are bassets. Wherever you live in England or Ireland there is certain to be a pack within easy reach, but there are few packs of beagles in Wales, and none at all in Scotland, to the best of my knowledge.

Mink hunting is a summer sport and has replaced otter hunting, which has ceased altogether in Great Britain although it still continues in Eire where the otter has not been driven out by pollution and poison and mink. Otter hunting used to be a great sport, especially on a big water. The mink does not supply sport of anything like an equivalent standard, but it can be fun on a pleasant summer's day, and the mink hounds do a useful job of controlling a right vicious little killer.

What sort of hunting you finally take to will really be a case of suck it and see. It is probably better to start quietly and feel your way, than to start with an expensive bang and then discover that you do not like it after all.

You would be very well advised to get your spouse interested in your chosen sport. Non-hunting spouses tend to get pretty sour about expenditure of time and money on hunting when they think that both commodities would be better wasted on them.

CONTACTING A HUNT

Once the chosen form of hunting has been decided on, the next question is how to actually join in. If you decide to follow

Three Counties minkhounds moving off from the meet at Foy, near Ross on Wye

foxhounds on foot, or in a car, there is no problem; you simply find out where the meet is and turn up. Simply may be an over simplification. At one time most hunts published their fixtures in the sporting magazines and the local press. However as the activities of the saboteurs have become increasingly violent, so hunts have become more reluctant to advertise. By the same token, hunt staff are very wary about dishing out information on the telephone to people whom they do not know. You may have to poke about a bit to find the information that you require, or you can write to the master or hunt secretary and state your case; it is the better thing to do anyway. When you go out with a pack for the first time do not expect the assembled company to surround you, shaking your hand and slapping your back. Hunt followers have learnt to be suspicious of people they do not know, and they will want time to weigh you up. But you will find that people will come and talk to you during the day; they will want to find out who you are, and the best advice is to be frank, and explain that you are a beginner. You will find plenty of people only too willing to unravel the mysteries of the chase for you; as a rule of thumb, the people who know least about hunting do the most talking about it.

To start hunting on a horse is rather more complex. If you have been learning to ride, your riding school or club should be able to advise you. If they cannot, try to find some established local hunting person who can. What you should not do is just turn up at a meet on your horse. It is important to remember, right from the start, that wherever you go out hunting, you are a guest on someone else's land. Those set in authority over the hunt have the responsibility to the landowners for the behaviour of those who follow the hunt. It can be a heavy responsibility, and the lads in head office like to know just what they are taking about with them. Not to put too fine a point on it, if you are the sort of guest who is going to get drunk and smash up the furniture, then they do not want you to come to their party. The thing to do is to write to, or otherwise contact the secretary of the hunt with whom you wish to disport yourself, and try to establish your bona fides. Be under no illusions but that he will immediately set in train investigations about you, and consult the master with his findings. No hunt is going to clasp to its collective bosom anyone who is likely to make trouble for it. I have refused to accept prospective subscribers because of their poor behaviour record but, as a beginner, you should have a clean slate.

The other problem that you may encounter is that many hunts have reached saturation point, the number of people that it is possible to take hunting in any given country being finite. Many hunts have a waiting list of would be subscribers, and if the hunt of your choice is in this position you will have to look elsewhere. It is the smarter hunts, with the better countries, that tend to have waiting lists, and they are not very suitable

places to cut your teeth in anyway. Start somewhere cosy and work up, if you so wish, as your expertise increases.

Hunting people are friendly and helpful on the whole, but it has to be said that this does not apply to everyone. There are also certain hunts where internecine feuding is endemic, and pursued with relish. These feuds are usually family based and their origins are lost in the mists of time, but that does not stop each successive generation pursuing the quarrel with all the enthusiasm of the Montagues and Capulets. If there is no very good reason for you to hunt in such a country then do not; remember what tends to happen to innocent bystanders in times of civil strife.

Different types of hunting, and different types of country suit different people. Try to find a country and a hunt that suits you, and where you are happy. Shop around a bit if you can. Remember all the time that hunting is supposed to be pleasure and that you are there to enjoy yourself. Whether you hunt on horse or foot, you will meet a lot of very interesting people and mostly welcoming from all walks of life. Whether or not you continue to be welcome will be entirely up to you.

4
Horses and Hounds

THE HORSE

This chapter is not going to be a treatise on horse mastership. If you should wish to read technical books about horses and the riding of them, there are any amount of excellent books on the subject. Forests of conifers have been pulped to supply the need that people feel to read about matters equine. Whole sections of bookshops are devoted to the horse, and hundreds of expert people have written hundreds of thousands of expert words on the matter. I have never read any of them, so am unable to recommend any.

It is very likely that it is the love of the horse that has brought you to teeter on the brink of hunting. I approached the matter from the opposite end: it was love of hunting that drove me to the horse. I like riding good horses because they convey me to hounds better than bad horses do. I never go near a horse except on hunting days, and the nearest I come to looking after a horse is to hand the animal's reins to the groom at the end of the day. I thought it only fair to tell you all this, so that what follows may be put in perspective.

The type to choose

This purports to be a book on hunting and, up to the time of this passage being written, the horse is the best method that has been discovered of following certain types of hound; as such it is worthy of consideration. And, if you want to go hunting, it follows that the sort of horse that you need is a hunter. Whilst all hunters are horses, by no means all horses make hunters.

Before anyone even considers hunting on a horse, they should acquire at least a modest competence in riding. You may think that this is stating the obvious, but it is an obvious that needs stating. Go to a competent riding school, and do not think of setting hoof in the hunting field until your competent instructor considers you too to be competent. Always remember that mounted hunting is a risk sport. If you tackle it unprepared, you will be a menace, and not only to yourself. You are also likely to hurt somebody else, or at least spoil their day's sport, if they have to stop and try to reassemble your constituent parts.

The ideal horse to start hunting on is an experienced old hunter who enjoys hunting and who will take you, and look after you, without frightening you; what is known in the trade as a 'patent safety', or a 'schoolmaster'. They are not easy to find, but are well worth taking some trouble to track down, and worth paying a bit for when you do find one. It is always worth paying a little more than you really want to for the right horse. You have only one neck, and you should consider what its intact state is worth to you.

A half-bred type of horse is suitable for most provincial countries. A half bred is usually assumed to be out of a draught mare by a thoroughbred, but there are variations on the theme. As a general rule the half bred tends to the common. It is slow, unemotional, will lumber about when it is required to, and in moments of inactivity will be quite happy to stand browsing off a hedge whilst you sip your flask and gossip to the person next to you. This is a sweeping generalisation, of course. There are some utterly foul half breds and a few, a very few, who have

The schoolmaster horse

the heart and soul of a Gold Cup horse; neither category is suitable for a beginner.

A lot of half breds are very good, safe jumpers, but very few can gallop; they tend to inherit their action from their plebeian ancestors. As you get more experienced, and desire better hunting, you will want better horses to cope with it. Common horses tend to be 'one pace', that is to say their engines are governed down; they will stay reasonably well providing they are allowed to gallumph along at their own pace. This will not do in some of the better hunting countries, where you will need to be able to go up through the gears and even into overdrive. As a rule of thumb, the better the hunting country, the nearer the thoroughbred your horse will require to be, and the more experience you will require to have. There is nothing quite like

'Common horses cannot climb hills . . .'

going across country on a good blood hunter, but they are no more suitable for a beginner than a Porsche would be for a learner driver.

If you are fortunate enough to start your hunting in a hill country, then a common horse is not what you want. Common horses cannot climb hills, nor gallop safely down them. A bit of breeding is necessary for hill hunting, and best of all is a bit of pony blood, which usually gives surefootedness and stamina.

Making a purchase

Once you have established what sort of horse you require, you will have to acquire it. You are about to dip your toe into a shark infested sea. There are many more bad horses than good

ones, and it follows that those who find themselves in posses-
sion of the bad ones will be very interested in divesting themselves of the problem, at a profit for preference. *Caveat emptor*
(let the buyer beware) is a very sound legal maxim, especially
when it comes to dealing in horses. You must work on the basis
that everyone is out to stick you. Economy with the truth
when selling a horse is regarded as perfectly respectable by all
degrees of society. Indeed there are those who seem to be quite
incapable of telling the truth about a horse, and to whom the
chance of pulling a stroke appears to be more important than
doing good business. So, how to set about the purchase? There
are three main ways of buying: you can buy privately, buy
from a dealer, or go to an auction.

Beware of the advertisement. Horsy magazines have columns
of advertisements for horses for sale. Most of them are mean-
ingless. If you ring up to try and extract more information, the
vendor will tell you what he/she thinks you want to hear. It is
of no importance to him/her that you will drive 150 miles, on
icy roads, to look at a horse that bears absolutely no re-
semblance to the horse that was advertised, and which you
have asked about. The vendor works on the principle that if
you do not come and look you will not buy the horse; if you do
come and look there is always the chance that you are the
clown the vendor has been praying for.

If you do decide to go a long distance to look at a horse, do
some homework. Even if you do not know someone who lives
nearby, you will almost certainly find someone who does
know somebody in the area. Find out before you drive. You
will save yourself much petrol and frustration. It is far and
away better to find a horse locally, if you can. The animal is
easily seen, and there will be no shortage of people only too
happy to point out its minutest drawbacks.

There is always your friendly neighbourhood dealer. You
will have met him out hunting. You will have laughed with him
in the pub. He is undoubtedly one of the most charming and
amusing men you have ever met. He is longing to help you. He

is longing to remove an arm and a leg from you for a three-legged mule. When you complain, he will be so charming and amusing that you will quickly realise that there is no way such a lovely man could have done anything dishonest. The long-standing and deep-seated diseases, from which your recently purchased horse is suffering, could not possibly have been known to the dealer when he sold the horse to you. Anyway, of course he will take the horse back and replace it. Of course you will understand that the replacement is a horse of much higher quality, and will cost you just a bit more than the original, but that is life, is it not? It is certainly horse dealing. Some dealers are more honest than others, and the better ones do have some sort of reputation to keep up, especially in their home district. If you use a dealer, find a local one, and find someone to help you of whom the dealer is frightened; there is such a person in every hunt.

Auction sales should be strictly no go areas to the novice. Remember that if the horse is any good, it is unlikely ever to go to auction. The only time I would buy a horse at auction is if it was a horse that I knew all about that was being auctioned for some good reason, a trustee sale for instance. I have sold a lot of horses at auctions and none of them have been any good. Auctions can be dustbins.

Horses are covered by the Trades Descriptions Act, which can give the purchaser some protection. I must confess that I have never heard of the Act being used successfully over a horse deal, but doubtless it has been. You should always have a horse vetted. Vets are very chary about warranting a horse sound these days because they too are subject to the Trades Descriptions Act, but they will tell you if there is some glaring defect that should preclude you buying the horse.

What should you look for when you go to inspect a prospective purchase? For a start, never go on your own. I have been buying horses for a quarter of a century, and I never go alone. Find a companion who really knows about horses, and whom the vendor recognises as someone who knows. Let the expert

do all the feeling, poking and prodding. You should stand still, keep quiet, betray no emotion except gloom, throughout the proceedings. Never laugh at the dealer's jokes, and not by so much as a flicker of an eyelid let him see that you like the horse. However there is one thing that the novice can see without any practice, and that is the horse's eye. A good horse will always have a kind, bold eye. A good eye looks the same in a horse as it does in a human being; if you are unable to tell the difference in either species, you are in deep trouble all round.

The other thing that the novice can notice is colour. The old saying is 'a good horse is never a bad colour', the rider to that is that a good colour does not necessarily denote a good horse. Colours to be doubtful about are very light bays and chestnuts, blacks, duns and coloured horses. A good dark bay, or brown, or iron grey (especially if you are not going to clean the horse yourself) are colours for consideration. Four white socks on a horse are supposed to be a danger sign.

The purchase of a horse is a very kittle business. Be cautious, and resist impulse buying, otherwise you will have plenty of time to repent. Any fool can buy a bad horse, but it takes an expert to sell one.

Once you have bought your horse, it will have to be clothed with saddle, bridle, rugs etc. What you will need will depend on circumstances, and you will require more expert advice than this book has room to give you, except for this: buy the very best that you can afford and look after it as though your life depended on it – one day it just might.

Riding to hounds

Riding to hounds; has little to do with the equitation which you will learn from those fierce ladies in stretch nylon breeches who run your local riding academy. It is quite possible that some of the things you read here will conflict with some of the things that you are taught by your BHSIs (British Horse Society Instructors). They are concerned with pure equitation, with a bias towards showing and showjumping. If you are a

fine natural horseman, this section is, in fact, wasted on you; it is for the Coarse Rider – the bad horseman who nevertheless always gets there in the end.

The horse is not a machine. Its powers are finite. It has just so many miles, and so many fences, in its figurative pocket before it packs the job in. If you gallop your horse to a standstill in the morning, you will miss the good hunt in the afternoon. Always assume that hounds are going to make a 10-mile point in the afternoon, and ride your horse accordingly. Never jump a fence unless it is necessary. Never trot when you can walk, and never gallop when you can trot. Any fool can knacker a horse in a couple of hours; the art lies in learning to save its powers for later. A horse will obviously travel faster and better on old grass than it will through hock-deep plough. Do not be impatient, set your pace according to your horse and the conditions.

It is possible that Pat and Sharon, at the riding school, will have taught you that riding by grip, with your foot right home in the stirrup iron, is right out of date, and so it may be in the show ring; out hunting, grip will save your neck. If you scoff at this reactionary statement, just try coming over a hairy fence with a 12-foot drop, riding their way. When you have picked yourself up, and someone has caught your horse, try it the old-fashioned way and find, to your surprise, that your horse remains where it should be – between your legs. Let us now consider some of the situations that the Coarse Rider may encounter out hunting.

Jumping   A good horseman will thoroughly understand how to place a horse at a fence. The Coarse Rider will not, and therefore by far the best thing to do is to leave the horse alone and allow it to make its own arrangements; it is far less likely to make a horlicks of the leap than you are. If the horse's own arrangement consists of regularly refusing to jump, you should change it for a bolder animal.

Different types of obstacle need to be tackled in different

'"Fly" fences need to be flown . . .'

ways. Solid timber, stone walls and other solid upright fences are best approached steadily; use a collected canter, or even a trot. To attain height the horse needs to be able to get its hind legs under itself and jump off its hocks. The same can be said to apply to wire. Most sensible horses can be taught to jump wire; it merely requires an act of will on the part of the rider. Properly tensioned wire is said to be the same as solid timber; it will either snap when you hit it, or turn you and your horse bustle over apex. It is perhaps better left to more experienced riders.

Certain parts of the UK, and much of Eire, are partitioned with banks. These are earth mounds that may be narrow and faced with stone, or wide and chubby with a ditch on one or both sides. These days they tend to have a mini forest on the top, and to be liberally festooned with wire. The horse does not fly a bank, it jumps onto the top, pauses, and then jumps

Riders jumping a hedge with the Belvoir Hunt in Leicestershire

off the other side unless the other side comprises a muck midden or a man waving a double-breasted gun, in which case you have the option of turning round and going back from whence you have just come. If you go to hunt in a bank country, then ride a bank-country horse. When you are approaching a bank, limit your equitation to closing your eyes, gripping with your knees, and taking a good fistful of mane; leave the rest to the horse.

'Fly' fences need to be flown, as their name suggests. They are the standard thorn fence encountered in many parts of England; in many countries they tend to have a ditch on one, or both, sides. A certain amount of impetus is required to negotiate fence and ditch, in other words you will need a horse that can gallop on and spread itself, a bold horse, to whose nerve your own should be equal. It is probably inadvisable to start a hunting career in a flying country; regular recumbency beneath a horse, in a wet ditch, tends to dampen enthusiasm.

Parts of the country have their fields separated by open ditches, or water-filled rhynes. A horse will jump a great width from a standstill, but wider waters require impetus. Ride a horse that is used to water, otherwise you will both get very wet learning about it. Many rhynes cover bottomless primeval ooze. If you get your horse in one you will need strong men, ropes and probably a tractor to extract it. If you happen to be underneath it, you will be past worrying about that anyway.

Gates are for opening, and *shutting*. If you jump a gate and break it, you will normally be expected to pay for it. The cost of a 10-foot field gate is £75, at the time of writing.

Hill country Hill hunting has charm, and problems all its own. It is very easy to pump out a horse on the hills, and there are certain basic principles to follow. Always let a horse go up-hill at its own pace; never push it. Once you have attained the summit, you may go down the other side as fast as your nerve will allow. There is an old West Country saying that 'it is easier to ride round the rim of the bucket, than over the handle'. In

other words, it is better to go round a declivity than down and up the other side, wherever this is feasible.

In most hill countries you will encounter stretches of wet ground. Some hills are wetter than others. For instance 'on Dartmoor you cannot ride anywhere, except where you can, whilst on Exmoor you can ride anywhere, except where you can't'. A good hill horse will skitter over a wet surface, but if you do sink, get off at once, and encourage your horse to better ground. Whatever you do, do not let it lie there and sulk; some horses will just give up. If it will not move, you will have to hit it. Getting a horse out of the 'stuggy' is a job for experts. If in doubt, in bad going, look for the tracks of sheep and cattle. They spend all their lives on a particular bit of hill, and have long since discovered the safe routes over bad ground.

It may happen that you get lost on the hill, fog can come down very suddenly and cause total disorientation. There is one certain way out of this situation: remember, every stream runs into a river, and every river runs into the sea, eventually.

All of this is very general, and quite frankly you will have to make mistakes, and learn by them.

Falling off It would be wrong to leave the subject of the horse without considering falling off it. Anyone who goes hunting on a horse is going to part company with his mount from time to time, and you must accept this fact. The important thing is to learn how to fall. Get some National Hunt racing on your video, and watch the jockeys; they have to know how to do it. The best possible thing is to find someone who is proficient at judo, and get him to teach you how to fall. Then practise it until it becomes automatic. You will bruise your shoulders, but one day it may save your neck.

HOUNDS

The two most fascinating animals in the world are the foxhound and the collie dog; that is a subjective opinion, but

The Tynedale hounds clearing a big wall in Northumberland

none the less sincere for all that. You will notice that one is a hound and the other a dog. The canine tribe is divided into two parts: hounds and curdogs. Hounds are foxhounds, harriers, beagles, otterhounds, bassets, and the various variations thereof. Everthing else is a curdog, including your Crufts champion, your brother's very expensive gundog, and all the rest. A hound is never a dog, and vice versa.

On the whole, hounds are animals of great charm and intelligence, but you must never lose sight of the fact that they have been bred with great care, over a very long time, to hunt and to kill, and that is what a good hounds wants to do most of all in his life. It is capable of tremendous affection and loyalty to the man who gives it sport, but a hound is not a pet, and is nearer the wild state than the average domestic animal. Hounds should always be handled with respect; get them wrong and

they can be savage. It is probable that every foxhound kennel in England has a story of the kennelman who went into the kennel in the dark to stop a fight, and all that was found in the morning were his boots and his bowler hat. It is quite certain that this did happen somewhere, but it is not all that common.

To succeed with hounds it is necessary to be a 'dog man'. Doggyness is innate, it cannot be acquired however hard you try. Hounds know as soon as you walk through the kennel door for the first time, whether you are the sort of chap that they are going to do business with, or not. If you are not, it matters not how much time you spend with them, and how much affection you lavish on them, they will not work for you. The bond between a good huntsman and his hounds verges on the uncanny, empathy is the appropriate word; in the hunting world it is called 'the thread'.

The technicalities of handling hounds are vast and complex, and much has been written about them. If you want more first-hand stuff, any huntsman given the chance, and maybe just the tiniest drop of whisky, will talk to you about it until your eyes glaze over, or the bottle is finished. It is enough for the beginner to know that hounds are the things you follow out hunting, and that their persons must be regarded as inviolable. However, it will be much more interesting to know a little more. There are several different types of hound hunting the fox in Great Britain. The main ones are the Old English, the Modern (or Standard), the Welsh, the Fell, and the West Country harrier. There are interminglings of these types, and there are esoteric variations such as bloodhound/French crosses and Kerry beagles, which are, to make it even more complicated, not beagles at all.

In the early part of this century the foxhound went through a bad patch. The foxhunting establishment was controlled by some terrifying old men who were past their active best and who became obsessed with the physical perfection of the hound to the detriment of its hunting qualities. There was a craze for massive bone and absolute straightness in the foreleg,

which had to knuckle over at the knee. The ideal was described as a square box with a straight leg at each corner. All very fine if you wanted a hound for standing in a corner and putting a vase of flowers on, but totally useless for catching foxes. Some of the younger masters rebelled against this fashion. They went to the less fashionable kennels where the good old blood lines were maintained and fashion had been denied entrance. They also went to unheard of places, like Wales, which had never heard of fashion. They started breeding a lighter, racier hound that could gallop and stay; some said it was a new type, others that they were trying to revive the type that maintained before what they referred to as the 'shorthorn era'. The shorthorn breeders were not amused, and civil war broke out in the foxhunting world. There are echoes of strife to this day. The Young Turks gradually gained the upper hand, and the foxhound you are most likely to encounter today is the type they laid the foundations of in the 1920s.

The Old English survives, just. I hasten to add that the examples that do remain are nothing like the grotesques that would have been hailed as beauties pre-1914. They do still tend to be heavier in frame and darker in colour than their Modern counterparts, and they command great devotion from their partisans. At the time of writing there are five packs of pure Old English hounds remaining. Pure in this context means that no outside breeding influences have been allowed to intrude into the pedigrees.

One of the major influences in the production of the Modern foxhound was the Welsh hound, a fact that many modern breeders find it convenient to forget. The pure Welsh is different in many ways to the English hound. It tends to be smaller and lighter, with a high domed skull and low set pendulous ears. It also tends to be rough coated, although in the same litter you can see every variation from satin smooth to shaggy. The origin of these hounds is almost certainly French, and legend has it that they are descended from hounds imported by the monks of Margam Abbey in the thirteenth

Welsh X hounds

century. That is not the whole story, as many of the good English lines went into Wales, and when the reformers were seeking to revive those lines they found them alive, and well, and living west of Offa's Dyke. The great thing about the Welsh hound was that it had been insulated from the dictates of fashion in its mountain fastnesses, and had only been kept for work. It would be nice if this was still the case, but sadly the Welsh have now been infected with the showing disease. A man visited a well-known Welsh kennel and saw two different sets of hounds, one tired and asleep on their benches after a hard day the day before, the other sleek, fat and shiny. Why the difference? Well there's a silly Saxon question. One lot were the hunting hounds, the others were kept for the showing in summer. There's a pity, in my opinion.

The Fell is another hound that was saved from fashion by its remote existence. It had its being, as it has today, on the

Scottish Borders and in north Yorkshire. It is a light framed racy hound and, like the Welsh, has great nose and tongue, independence and toughness. It needs all these qualities to catch the wild hill foxes on the Border crags.

The trouble with all the hill breeds is that they tend to be nervous and easily upset; they require sensitive handling, and hate being pressed on, or ridden over, which is why they tend not to be suitable for the more fashionable countries. The Old English hound, after having been galloped over by a hundred horses, will pick itself up, shake itself and carry on.

Nevertheless, the qualities of the hill hounds have been recognised by thoughtful breeders over the years, who have found an infusion of hill blood beneficial in their low country strains.

The West Country harrier is found mainly in the west of England, as its name implies. It is a small lemon and white hound which was originally bred for harehunting. There are more harrier packs in the west than anywhere else in England, but, just to make it all more complicated, they mostly now hunt fox. It I had to choose· a single type of hound, I would choose the West Country harrier; for me it is the rough country hound of greatest excellence.

The 'Stud Book' harrier is the usual harehunting harrier. It tends to look like a smaller Standard foxhound. There are probably only fifteen packs of such harriers in England, so they are not often met with.

Beagles and bassets are, as mentioned in Chapter 3, the hounds used by foot packs to hunt hares. Probably everyone knows what the jolly little beagle looks like. And although dedicated beaglers conduct endless esoteric arguments about the different types of beagle, the fact is that one beagle is pretty much like another. You will probably also recognise a basset if you see one. The hunting basset tends to be rather more streamlined than the showbench variety. All breeds of animals are ruined by competitive showing, and the basset has been no exception. The hunting type has been refined by doses of beagle blood, to make it more practical. There have also been

experiments with French Griffon Vendéen blood. These hounds have broken coats, and rumour has it that they possess a marked Gallic instability of temperament.

There used to be a pure breed of English staghound, but it died out during the the last century and all the hounds hunting deer in the British Isles are now of foxhound origin.

The pure bred otterhound still exists to hunt mink. It is a comparatively young breed in this country, going back less than a hundred years and probably having a French Nivernais Griffon base. The otterhound is very shaggy, has a tremendous voice, but a poor constitution; wherefore it has been increasingly supplanted by foxhound-bred hounds.

If you wish to get really interested in your local hounds, you will find most huntsmen only too pleased to welcome true enthusiasts. The more that you learn about hounds and hunting, the more you will enjoy your sport. However it is also fair to say that 80 per cent of those who hunt know as little about hounds when they give up as they did when they started, so it is obviously possible to enjoy hunting from a position of blissful ignorance.

5
Dress and Behaviour

DRESS

There are three important considerations as regards hunting clothes: they must be warm, comfortable and well presented. Let us consider the last first. Whatever kind of hunting you may decide to take up, you should always present yourself at the meet, in a tidy state. It matters not that you will shortly be torn, bedraggled and bespattered with mud. By beginning in good order you are showing respect for those who hunt with you, and for those over whose land you are going to hunt; it is a question of good manners. This does not mean that all your kit has to be built for you in Savile Row, it merely means that whatever you wear should be clean and neat.

Warmth is all-important. Few people are currently accustomed to prolonged exposure to the British winter weather. It would be a pity to start a hunting career with hypothermia. Start from the inside, with good warm underclothes. Thermal garments are very warm, but tend to smell. A woollen shirt should come next, and then sweaters or waistcoats to taste. Most people tend to wear nylon breeches these days. They are

very flattering to the contours but very cold, so wear plenty underneath; twill or cord breeches are much better. The coat is extremely important. A good hunting coat is a good investment. All too often beginners come out hunting in little summer showing coats that they buy at the local pony shop; these are totally useless. A good thick wool cloth coat, with thick lining, is the thing, it will keep you warm even when wet. A waterproof overcoat is a matter for personal choice, although the harder-bitten hunting people frown on them for aesthetic reasons. There are practical reasons against them too; they are bulky and restricting, and whilst they may keep the rain out they also keep the condensation in, so the net benefit is nil.

For long hours of walking or riding, comfort is essential. This means that whatever you wear must fit, and allow you all necessary movement. If you are a standard size, you may be able to kit yourself off the peg, which makes it all much cheaper. The alternative is to have your clothes built for you, which is expensive. But remember that you get what you pay for. Well made clothes will last longer, fit better, and look better; they are a good investment. You do not have to go to London for your hunting clothes. There are several excellent regional tailors who specialise in this type of work. I have had my hunting clothes made by various mail order firms for many years. Again there are specialist mail order companies who make to measure at a fraction of the price that you would pay in Savile Row.

The mounted hunter

What to wear, and when, is a complicated matter for the mounted hunter. There are three main forms of dress, and it is important to get them right; they are: 'ratcatcher', black coat, and red coat.

Ratcatcher consists of brown, or black butcher boots, spurs, drab breeches, tweed coat, collar and tie or coloured stock tie, and bowler hat or, more likely, a hunting cap, these days. I ex-

Two well-turned-out riders

pect all that sounds like a load of gibberish, so we'll do the right thing – start at the bottom and work our way up.

Butcher boots are the plain leather or rubber boot. They are usually black. Rubber boots are cheaper and easier to clean. They are also clammy, and do not give the protection to the leg that leather does. There is a compromise. You can get French rubber boots that are lined with leather. They are made to measure and cost more, but are well worth considering. Made to measure boots of good quality leather are now so expensive as to be beyond the reach of all but the very rich. Cheaper leather boots are available but, with leather, you get what you pay for. Good quality second-hand boots are often a possibility, consult your local saddler. You should always wear a garter strap with your boot. This is a little strap that goes through a loop at

the back of the boot and buckles below the knee, with the strap-end facing outwards. To stop it riding round the knee, cut a little slit in the strap, and put it on the second button from the top on the knee of the breeches. The garter strap serves no useful purpose these days, but no boot looks right without one. Spurs should always be worn out hunting. Ask your saddler for a pair of 'Prince of Wales' spurs and straps, and get him to show you how to put them on.

Drab breeches are merely any other colour than white. A tweed coat is a tweed coat, and a collar and tie is just that. A stock tie is a very different thing altogether. It is basically a strip of cloth, usually shaped, which is wound twice round the neck, tied in the front, and pinned. Well tied, it looks very smart; badly tied it looks like a pudding cloth; practice some-

A Prince of Wales spur, and properly fitted spur and garter strap

Ratcatcher

times makes perfect. The stock tie should always be tied tightly, for two very good reasons. If it is tight it will give your neck some measure of support in a fall, and it will stop the rain running down your neck.

Bowler hats were originally designed by a Norfolk gentle-man to protect the heads of his gamekeepers from the cudgels of the poachers. Now they have come down in the world. They are excellent for keeping the rain off the neck, but as a skull protector the modern bowler is totally useless. The hunting

cap, or the fibre-glass crash hat with a cover, is now almost universal in the hunting field. There has been controversy over chin straps. It is a matter of personal choice as to whether you decide to wear one. If you wear a properly made and fitted hunting cap, you will not need a chin strap. The only firm who hand make, and fit, hunting caps is Patey of Amelia Street, London. If you are just going to buy one off the peg from the local saddler, then get a chin strap too.

Ratcatcher is worn during cubhunting. It is also usually worn in April where a pack is fortunate enough to be able to go on into spring. You would also normally wear it for staghunting.

Black coat The hunting season formally opens with the Opening Meet, and formal dress is the order of the day from then on. You should start hunting in a black coat. The classic hunting coat is a 'body coat', which is just the technical name for the way it is cut. If your tailor has never heard of a body coat, you are wasting your time with him. You may have heard of swallow tailed coats for hunting; they are still worn, but only by swells in Leicestershire; you need a perfect figure and very well-bred horses to get away with tails. Your black coat should have three, or four, buttons at the front. The lady's black coat is cut rather differently but, once again, your tailor or purveyor should know enough to advise you. It is perfectly possible, and respectable, to buy second-hand coats. The older the coat, the better quality the cloth is likely to be. Modern cloth does not compare well with the pre-1939 article.

With the black coat you should wear black boots, drab breeches, a white stock tie and, until recently, you would have worn a top hat or a bowler. We have discussed the demise of the latter, the top hat is an equally endangered species. The proper silk hat has almost ceased to exist except among old-fashioned swells, who still cling to them and know the difficult art of caring for them, or have a man who does. The top hat may be discounted for anyone currently taking up hunting.

Top hat

Most hunts now allow all followers to wear some form of hunting cap, a grey one appears to be the modern norm for men, and blue, or black, for women. The black hunting cap, with a black coat, has for long been the traditional dress of the hunting farmer. In many hunts, the farmers guard their sartorial preserve with a certain amount of passion. The best thing is to take advice as to the dress customs that prevail in your particular hunt.

The red coat   Now the red coat; not a scarlet coat, and never a

Hunt servant or master

pink coat. Hunting pink only exists in the tabloid press. You wear a red coat, or you wear scarlet (without the coat).

You should not set yourself up in a red coat to begin with. It should only be worn with a hunt button, that is the distinctive button of your hunt. The hunt button is only within the gift of the master, and is awarded like colours at school. You may wear a plain button on a red coat if you are a serving officer in HM Forces. Many people stick to their black coat even when they have the hunt button, it is much easier to clean. With the red coat you will probably wear a hunting cap these days, but

the black cap is only worn by hunt officials.

A white stock tie is normal, although you will see some aged toffs who still wear a blue bird's-eye stock tie. These went out of general wear before World War I, but they are still correct if you have the style to carry them off.

White breeches are the norm, but not essential. Top boots are essential, and white (clean) garter straps with white breeches. The top boot is a black boot with a coloured leather top below the knee. The origin was the old thigh boot as per your Laughing Cavalier. In fine weather the boot would be turned down below the knee (like waders) and secured to the knee with a strap – the now redundant, but correct, garter strap. The inside lining of the thigh boot tended to be of brown leather, and the whole cumbersome thing eventually evolved into the top boot, which became the normal riding boot of the Georgian and Victorian country gentleman, the man who would have normally worn a red coat for hunting.

You may say that all these dress codes are anachronistic rubbish, and you would have a point. You may also say that they are part of the continuing traditions of the English countryside, and you could score with that as well. I suggest that they are all part and parcel of hunting, and that no one is forcing you to join.

It cannot be overstressed that whatever you wear should fit you properly. If you have never had the experience, you will have no idea of the havoc that a badly fitting pair of breeches can cause to all sorts of strange portions of the anatomy. By the same token, when buying a coat, remember that you will not always be wearing it to admire yourself in the looking-glass at the shop, you want to be able to move in it as well; it is a coat, not a strait jacket.

Vanity and boots are an ill-matched pair. Do not have boots that are too tight in the leg, or the instep. You want to be able to get them on, and off, with reasonable ease, and you want room in the foot for an extra pair of socks.

The Middleton hacking on to draw

Accessories   You will need some sundries of equipment. You will need a pair of metal hooks to get your boots on, and a boot-jack to pull them off. Tight leather boots are the very devil to get off when wet. If you cannot get them off with the jack, it is a job for your valet in his green baize apron. If you have not got a valet, it is a job for a loved one, and there is a knack to it. Sit in an armchair; get the loved one facing away from you with the offending boot between his/her legs. The Loved One should grasp the heel of the boot in one hand, and the toe in the other, pulling the heel and pushing the toe simultaneously. At the same time you should place the other foot flat on the Loved One's posterior, and push whilst trying to pull the other leg out of the boot. You may think I jest, but I assure you that this is the tried and trusted way of removing a difficult boot; just do not expect the Loved One to get to like it.

A flask is a comforting thing to take hunting; even if you do not drink yourself, you will find that the master will seldom refuse a dram.

You should always carry a whip out hunting (it is never a crop). The whip should always have a thong and a lash. The traditional hunting whip is very useful for opening gates, that is why it has a crook at the end. Your whip is not for cracking, or flicking at hounds with; make a practice of that and you will quickly find yourself lifted in such a way as you thought had gone out with sergeant majors and national service.

You will see that certain people carry wire-cutters on their saddles. You should not set up a pair unless asked to do so by the master. For very obvious reasons the latter are pretty touchy about wire-cutters in unreliable hands.

I would advise anyone to carry a spare stirrup leather. You can either put this around your horse's neck, where it makes a very convenient strap to hang on to, or coil it up and hang it on one of your saddle Ds. I have only had three leathers break in thirty years, but those were three hunts that I would have lost without a spare.

Tips   It is assumed that you do not have anyone to do your valeting for you, so some tips may be valuable.

The nap on a velvet cap may be brought up by steaming it gently over a kettle spout, and then brushing with a soft brush.

The disadvantage of a red coat is that it has to be scrubbed every time you wear it. Rainwater is always supposed to be the best to use. There are proprietory preparations for cleaning red coats and removing the stains that increase with age, but I have my doubts about them. Brass buttons should always be polished, and you will need a button stick to stop the polish getting on the cloth.

Most breeches can be washed in a machine, whatever your tailor says.

Rubber boots are dead easy; just wash them off, and use furniture polish when dry.

Leather boots need looking after. Always wash them off as soon as you get home. Put the first coat of polish on when they are still damp. When they are dry put on more polish, and

brush up. Use a good quality wax polish, and never oil your boots if you want them to shine again.

Very few people have the time, or inclination, to bone their hunting boots these days, but it is the proper way to look after good ones, and the only way to have them really immaculate. If you are fortunate enough to be able to buy the sort of boots that are worth boning, either hire a man to do them for you (no one under forty-five will know how), or get your bootmaker to show you how to do it. Do not buy a bone from your boot-maker, he will sell you a clean, boiled, polished article which is very expensive and useless. What you need is the leg bone of a deer from which the flesh has been allowed to rot away naturally. The bone contains all the natural grease which will do your boots good. Get a fresh one every year, although it is possible that fresh is not the correct word in this particular context.

The foot hunter

What of the foot hunter? His needs are nothing like as complicated, but the three criteria of warmth, comfort, and presentation still apply.

A good pair of boots is all-important. What kind of boots you care to use for walking or running is up to you and your feet, and you should try various types until you find the one that suits you. Again the principle of getting what you pay for applies, and good walking boots are expensive, but worth every penny. Rubber boots should be avoided. They give the foot no support, and are cold and clammy.

Remember that plenty of layers of natural fibre are the best thing. Accept the fact that you are going to sweat and get wet. You want clothing that will not allow condensation, but that will keep you warm when you are soaked. Simply getting wet will not do you a lot of harm, sitting about in wet clothes will. If you have a long drive in prospect after hunting, have some dry clothes in your car.

Plus-fours, or knickerbockers, are the finest things for walk-

ing in though you may be a little hesitant about wearing such anachronistic garments. It is true that if you were to march down some suburban high street in plus-fours, you might excite comment. However, where you are going the style of everyday dressing has hardly changed in fifty years; plus-fours and hairy stockings will be regarded as quite normal.

The other thing that the foot hunter should invest in is a good stick. A stout 'horn heid' shepherd's stick is a good investment, and will quickly become an old friend.

Every hunter should carry a good (sharp) knife, some string and some money; you will find need for all of them from time to time.

It is no bad thing to do some first-aid training. Hunting is dangerous, and yet surprisingly few people who hunt have any knowledge of first aid. I remember a certain hunt that boasted a doctor, a dentist, a vet and a priest amongst its followers; but not all hunts are similarly blessed.

BEHAVIOUR

Most hunting behaviour and etiquette is merely an extension of everyday good manners and common sense. It has to be said that common sense is by no means as common as it might be, and a whole post-war generation has been taught that good manners equate with bourgeois liberalism and are therefore wrong. It must also be said that many people possessed of good manners, and good sense, allow these to temporarily evaporate as soon as they get on a horse. Remember that to get on a horse and go hunting is a great privilege, and confers no rights at all; it certainly does not confer the right to be ill mannered, indeed there is a positive duty to be even more gracious than you usually are.

When out hunting: speak. If you are hacking on to the meet, say 'good morning' and be pleasant to everybody you meet on the road. If a car slows down for you, salute it. If someone opens a gate for you, say 'Thank you'. You may say that you

would do this as a matter of course; I wonder. I once saw a farmer open his own gate to let a hunt through his own yard; a hundred people rode past him without so much as looking at him. If I had been he I would have warned them off, and in fact a hunt was warned off a 600-acre farm recently for precisely this lack of manners, and serve them right. Never forget that wherever you go out hunting you are somebody's guest. The man in the dirty wellies and the old brown smock is your host, and could probably buy and sell you twice over; be civil to him.

Even the highway belongs to the Queen; she wants all her subjects to have beneficial use of it; she does not want you blocking her road with your horse. There is nothing more annoying, if you are in a hurry, than to find your way blocked by an impervious mass of steaming horses and chattering humanity. It annoys me, and I am a hunting man; it makes non-hunting people into anti-hunting people. Rule 1 is: Do Not Block Roads.

Rule 2 is: Shut All Gates. If you are a farmer, you will be aware of the importance of this. If you are not a farmer you will be back in your cosy office when your erstwhile host is wasting half a day sorting out the two lots of sheep that your careless-ness allowed to get mixed up. Such carelessness is sheer bad manners, may be expensive to the farmer, and may well get the hunt denied access to that farm. Gates, and the stock that may escape through them, are a constant worry to those responsible for a day's hunting, and everyone who hunts must make these things their worry too. It is so easy in the heat of the moment to say to yourself that there is someone else coming behind who will shut the gate; unless you are absolutely sure that this the case, it is your duty to do it. There is a tried system for gates. When you have opened one, or come to an open one, stop and look behind you; if you see someone coming, raise your hand and wait until he acknowledges your signal; once he has done so, he has accepted responsibility for the gate and you may gallop on with a clear conscience.

Never allow your horse to kick hounds

Gates are not the only way that stock may escape; a hole in the hedge will do just as well. If you have broken a fence, tell someone in authority as soon as possible. In many stone-wall countries it is the custom that, if you knock a wall down, you stop and put it up again.

Do not gallop through stock and get them overexcited. You would not want your heavily pregnant wife scoused about. Look at every cow as though she was your wife.

Always get out of the way of the hunt staff. They have a job to do; if you impede their progress, you will get bellowed at, and will receive absolutely no sympathy for your bruised ego. Whatever you do, do not allow your horse to kick a hound, hounds are sacred; harm one, and the sky will fall on you. Remember that hounds are brought up to trust horses, and that a bad kicker can kill or maim. A horse that kicks should not be brought out hunting. Most can be cured of kicking by getting a right good hiding when they do it, but let them learn on your own family and dogs, not on innocent strangers, human and canine, out hunting. If hounds are coming past you in a narrow

place, as in a lane, always turn your horse's head towards them; very few horses kick successfully with their front end.

It is not uncommon these days to find a hound hung up in a wire fence, with a leg fast between the two top strands. It is your duty to free it. It is best done by two, for the hound will almost certainly try to bite. Let one of you give it a whip to chew whilst the other hauls it back over the fence, thereby untwisting the leg.

Learn to differentiate between old grass, new leys and winter corn. They are all green, but there the similarity ends. No one will blame you for not knowing, but they will blame you for not trying to find out.

There are not many countries where people can take their own line across country these days. Even where it is possible, many people like to tuck in behind a good goer and let him soften up the fences for them. There is no sin in this. The great sin in jumping is to follow someone too closely over a fence. If your pilot falls and you jump on him, you may kill or cripple, which is probably not at all what you have in mind.

The best place to jump a fence is where it looks biggest and blackest; horses will treat it with respect. Most bad falls take place over washy little fences which horses have been too flippant with. Once you have chosen your jumping spot, go for it; do not suddenly change your mind and cut across someone else's bows – at best, you will have your pedigree recited unto you; at worst, you will be involved in a nasty smash.

If a person gets off to open an awkward gate, it is customary for those who have benefited from the kindness to wait until he/she has shut the gate and remounted. It is not the thing to gallop off leaving the unfortunate hopping about with one foot in the stirrup iron; it might be your turn next time, and just see how you like it.

A word about tipping may be in order. Many people do not come much in contact with gratuities these days, what with service charges and all. In the hunting world you will still find traces of personal service. The hunt staff are deemed to be the

personal servants of the masters; many people still have grooms, and there is still the odd (sometimes very odd) butler lurking about in the rural deeps. It is customary to tip people who have performed a service for you. For instance, suppose you stay with a friend who also puts up your horse; you should always tip the groom – a tenner would be about right. Even if there is no obvious domestic help in the house, leave a fiver beside the bed; there may be a daily help. If there is a butler, you must press your offering into his hand; it should be crinkly (the offering, that is).

Whether you like it or not, and whether they admit it or not, when you are on a horse the dismounted public will regard you as a sample of the knightly caste; this will evoke respect from some, dislike from many others. However unknightly you may feel, it nevertheless behoves you to behave with the utmost chivalry whilst mounted. Never allow yourself to offend anyone unintentionally. If you feel an urge to be rude to somebody, follow the admirable dictum of Colonel Wintle that 'you should never be rude to anybody under the rank of full Colonel'. Full colonels are more than able to give as good, or better, than they get. Try it and you will find out.

6
The Hunting Year: Summer

Once the hunting season is over the various participants tend to go their separate ways, and for many of them the hunt ceases to exist during the summer months. This is not the case. The hunting season runs from 1 November to 30 April, and 'summer' starts on 1 May. It is not possible to wrap hounds up in tissue paper and stack them away in boxes until the next opening meet. There is a lot of work to be done in the summer, as well as a bit of time for relaxation after a long hard winter. So what do the various members of the cast get up to in summer?

Let us start with the master: these days, most masters have a farm or business to attend to, but hunt business has to go on. Summer is the time for repairs and maintenance. Let it be said again that hunting exists on goodwill, and much of that will depend on the master's personality. It is a good rule of thumb that every farmer, landowner and gamekeeper in a hunt country should be visited by the master at least once a year. There will be complaints to be solved and ruffled feathers to be soothed, but on the whole the master is a welcome visitor whose arrival is counted unto him for righteousness and will be occasion for

tea and cake, at the very least, and lots of chat. Sometimes the hospitality can be a little more vigorous. Masters doing their rounds in cider-making country will be expected to sample, and appear to enjoy, the local produce; this can be extremely tiring. All these visits have to be crammed into a fairly short space of time, missing out periods of maximum stress, like hay time and harvest, when visitors are not really welcome.

There will be physical maintenance to attend too as well. Rides have to be trimmed out, coverts maintained, hunt jumps repaired, and perhaps new ones put in. If the master hunts hounds himself, he will have to spend a lot of time at the kennels; hounds are like women, and do not take kindly to emotional neglect.

Most huntsmen will admit to letting out their belts a notch or two in summer, but the work goes on. A pack of hounds operates on a continuous cycle. Every year so many litters of puppies will be bred, normally between February and May. When the whelps are 8 to 10 weeks old, 'they go out to walk'. This means that get they go away from the kennels, usually to a farm, where they get the two Fs, food and freedom. They are allowed to roam and play and develop their minds and bodies, and receive the individual attention that would not be possible if they were all kept at the kennels. By the following spring all the puppies will be back at the kennels, and the next stage of their education will begin.

Hounds should spend as much time out of the kennels as possible in summer. During the early part, the staff will just waddle out on foot with them, wandering down the lanes and down to the river for a swim and a game. At this stage the young hounds will be on couples. A couple is simply two collars with a chain between. One collar goes on a steady old hound and the other on a young hound; in this way the young hound soon learns what the various commands mean, and will have a fairly painless introduction to good manners and discipline. As summer progresses, so the exercise tempo increases. The bicycles come out and, in late summer, the cobs. The daily

Hound exercise

distances will gradually increase so that, by the start of the autumn hunting, the hounds will be as hard and fit as exercise can make them.

But exercise is not just a route march, it is training as well. Hounds should be taken continuously through stock, farmyards and villages, and the young hounds must learn about cats, sheep and chickens. They must be given the chance to behave badly. When they do, punishment must be swift, exemplary, and hard. A young hound who chases a sheep when out on exercise, and gets a good hiding, will remember that lesson for the rest of his life. Failure to check the problem at that stage will mean an inevitable bullet later on. An unsteady pack of hounds is a mobile disaster area.

Exercise is not the only thing that occupies the hunt staff. The kennels have to be spring cleaned and painted, for cleanliness ranks next to godliness in a good kennels, and there are the

The puppy show

continuous kitchen chores to be attended to. A pack of hounds takes a lot of feeding. Their basic diet is meat and porridge. The porridge is fresh made daily. The meat supply comes from 'fallen stock'. Suppose that you are a farmer and you have a sheep, or a cow, die. When you have finished swearing and prophesying black ruin, you are faced with a disposal problem. Of course, you can dig a large hole, but you probably have better things to do, so what you really do is telephone the kennels, and shortly will appear an ancient Land Rover with a trailer with a winch on it. The carcass will be loaded. When the knacker wagon completes its run, and returns to the kennels, the carcasses are skinned, gutted, cut up, and put on the menu. It all takes time. If you want a rule of thumb, a good cow would feed ten couples of hounds for about a week.

Most hunt servants are welcoming to those who take a genuine interest in their hounds. If you take the trouble to learn a bit about the hounds, you will get more fun out of your hunting. If you really play your cards right, you may be allowed to help with the knackering and the skinning. Eviscerating a half rotten sheep, on a hot July day, may well assist you to develop a whole new philosophical approach to life.

The summer is not all stern duty, it is also show time. Every hunt has a puppy show, when the young hounds, who have been out at walk, are judged for conformation and movement by visiting experts. The main aim of the puppy show is to say thank you to the puppy walkers. Walking a hound puppy every year is no sinecure, and can be an expensive exercise in money and patience. Hound puppies have immense charm, but they are also immensely destructive, terrible gardeners, and born thieves. Even so the same people take them year after year, and sometimes generation after generation. The puppy show is also a great social occasion, with many visiting hunters. There is nearly always tea after the show, and speeches, and it is not unknown for a party to develop in the evening. It should be remembered that the puppy show costs money to put on. Who gets to go to it will depend pretty much on who pays for it: some are more private than others. You should find out what the custom is in your particular hunt, before the wife gets her Ascot hat out of the box.

There are also hound shows in summer. The bigger ones are usually attached to one of the big agricultural shows, the biggest one of all being Peterborough, which is part of the East of England show. Packs will come from a wide area to show their hounds at these shows, and they are well worth a visit. It will give you some idea of what a hound ought to look like, and to see some of the different types of hound. You will also see a lot of interesting people including men, and women, who are legends in their own lifetime. There will be time for a reviving glass or two with friends, and there will be a lot of gossip. The real purpose of hound shows should be the crack: the showing

The Dulverton East hounds at their kennels in Devon

of hounds should not be taken too seriously; a hound is not meant for hunting pots.

There are smaller local hound shows, which are certainly not serious. My favourite show takes place at a bleak moorland crossroads. There are a few sheep, a few hounds, and a produce show. There is also a corner of broken down wall across which a tarpaulin is stretched, to protect the vast quantity of Grouse Whisky that huddles there. The actual show takes no time at all; the après show takes a lot longer. The only reason for having the show there is the particular excellence of the local water when properly diluted.

Some hunting countries are fortunate in being able to start hunting in August, or even the end of July. Most countries have their start regulated by the harvest. If the harvest is late, it

may be the end of September, or into October, before a start can be made. By this time hounds and staff will be pig sick of exercising. In most countries there are only so many exercise routes available, and however you perm them, you get fed up with them. Many people join in with the mounted exercise occasionally, and thoroughly enjoy it, but if you do it 6 days a week for 7 or 8 weeks, then you will be very pleased to start hunting, which is exactly what we will do in the next chapter.

7

Autumn Hunting

To describe cubhunting, or autumn hunting as it is now usually referred to, I cannot do better than quote the words of Lord Willoughby de Broke in his excellent book *Hunting the Fox*:

> . . . the scientific direction of the Cubhunting is of crucial importance. It is here that the pack is made or marred. It cannot be too often repeated that the primary object of the Cubhunting is to teach the young Hounds to hunt, and in addition to complete the education of the last year's entry. Puppies are of no proven value to the pack during their first season, and cannot even begin to be counted as reliable until at least the end of their second Cubhunting. As well as training the young Hounds, the Cubhunting season gives opportunity and leisure to the Master and his Staff to study the science and to practise the art of the chase . . . Cubhunting should begin the very moment the state of the harvest will allow, and should be pursued relentlessly, no matter how hard the ground may be.

So now you know. Cubhunting is the master's private time, when the subscriber has no rights whatsoever. With the more traditional packs, you will still be expected to ask the master's permission before going out, and to do as you are told, and to make yourself useful when you get there. If you do not like it, you can always stay in bed, for cubhunting usually takes place in the early morning. For me it is a magical time. If you have never experienced the English countryside, at daybreak, on an autumn morning, then you truly have a treat in store. Add a pack of hounds and a litter of foxes to the scenario, and you are in for a feast of sights, sounds and smells. For all the years that I have been hunting, I never fail to thrill to that very special moment when the first whimper denotes the finding of the first fox of a new season.

There is a harder purpose to the cubhunting than just the education of young hounds, for implicit in that education is learning to kill foxes. Most fox cubs are born in the early spring. By the autumn they are fully grown, and already killing for themselves. An undisturbed litter will tend to stay around its base area, and this can lead to a density in a local fox population that may be unacceptable to the local human inhabitants. It should never be forgotten that the fox is a carnivore, and that he does not purchase his meat from the butcher; he goes out and slays it for himself. So there is a culling element in the cubhunting. The weaker cubs are killed and the stronger ones escape as is the way in nature.

HOW CUBHUNTING IS CONDUCTED

How cubhunting is conducted will vary according to the type of hunting country and the density of the fox population therein. The whereabouts of nearly all the litters will be known by late summer and, as soon as the harvest allows, hunting should begin.

It is vital to start where there is as much certainty as there can be of dropping on a litter of cubs quickly. There is nothing

A cubhunting morning

more destructive to the morale of young hounds than to spend two hours in a covert seeking a non-existent litter of cubs. The hounds are fit, keyed up, and raring to go; the old hounds will know that they are being taken hunting, and their excitement will infect the youngsters. That excitement is bound to find an outlet, and, if there is no legitimate quarry available, it is hardly surprising if youth finds something else to chase, with disastrous results all round. So the hunt staff must do their homework, and wherever is chosen for the first morning must have a resident litter.

It is the received wisdom amongst hound men that cubhunting is always best started in big woodlands, that young hounds should 'see no daylight' for the first month of the hunting. This is sensible. In a big woodland there is space to hunt. The old hounds can settle to their work, and the young hounds will quickly learn to join in the fun by using their ears and their noses, which is the way it should be with hounds. In the open there may be too many, all too visible, distractions, such as deer or hares, which may prove irresistible to headstrong

youth. Of course, these things will also be present in the coverts, but not so obviously visible, and therefore not so tempting. It should go without saying that the coverts chosen should be easily accessible for the hunt staff, so that they can nip incipient problems in the bud. Any master who is so foolish as to launch his young entry into a thousand acres of trackless forest, deserves all the trouble that will undoubtedly ensue; but, sadly, it is hounds who will end up being shot, when it should be the clown who got them into bother in the first place.

Not all countries have suitable, large woodland areas. There are parts of the country where small coverts abound, or where there are large areas of roots or kale. If this is the case, it may be necessary to 'hold up'. There may be good, more local, reasons for this as well, such as a field of uncut corn in the vicinity, or a wood full of young pheasants. We have already established that too much premature scousing about in the wild blue yonder may be harmful to the impressionable young. It is also certain that hard ground, and blind hedges, can be a recipe for writing off a horse for the rest of the season, or worse.

To hold up a covert, people are dispersed at strategic intervals around it, and at a suitable distance from it, with the brief of turning the foxes back into the covert. Holding up is a purely utilitarian operation, and should only be used where the situation demands it. If it is badly done, or done to excess, it becomes unacceptable and self defeating. I have seen hounds remain in a small covert surrounded with shouting people for four hours, and still not catch a fox. The reasons for this failure were quite simple. First, noise; bad noise has probably saved more foxes than almost anything else for it distracts hounds, especially young hounds, and breaks their concentration. The only sound they should be hearing is the cry of their elders and betters. Shouting gets hounds' heads up when they should be on the ground, smelling, which leads us to the second reason for the failure – foil. If hounds spend too long going backwards and forwards over the same ground, that ground becomes

foiled. This simply means that the whole covert will stink of hound, which will effectively mask the scent of the fox, especially as that scent becomes more elusive as the warmth of the autumn day increases. A covert foiled to this extent will be unlikely to hold a fox again for at least six weeks, so taking it all in all, it will be a bad morning's work that finishes up by doing no good to anyone.

If holding up is done, it should be done quietly; the tapping of a stick, or the clap of a hand, is often sufficient. It will not deter all the foxes. There is no human agency that will stop a really determined fox; I have seen them go between a man's legs. The old vixen will be the first to go, and nothing will stop her. The more determined cubs will go next, and good luck to them, they are the ones who will give good hunts later on. Most huntsmen will be content for their hounds to have killed two cubs out of a litter at the end of a hard morning, and it is best if this is done in good style, above the ground. However, if it means a dig, then that must be.

It is particularly important for the morale of hounds, at this crucial time of year, that their morning's work should come to an appropriate conclusion. To achieve this it is better to stick to one litter per morning. In autumn, if the weather is good, the best of the scent will be gone by 8 o'clock, and by 10 o'clock the scent will have evaporated altogether. The worst thing a huntsman can do, when things start to get difficult after two hours' hard work amongst a litter, is to cut away and start amongst fresh foxes with tired hounds. He will be leaving tired foxes behind him, so that a little more perseverance might well have got his hounds their reward. A lot of hunting is about perseverance, and this virtue in a hound has to be reinforced by perseverance in the huntsman. Even when all the scent is gone, and all seems lost, the huntsman should ask his hounds to try just once more; that is the time when a well-hunted cub may very likely come to hand. A fox well caught at the end of a hard morning has untold value in the shaping of the young hound.

There are many parts of the country where holding up is not

possible. There are places in the South West where the fields are divided by large hairy overgrown banks, and double hedges. These are often stuffed with foxes, and cubhunting here will be full of movement and excitement, and more fun than standing outside a covert for two or three hours. However let me stress again that cubhunting is a working time, and its primary object is to make the hounds who will provide fun later on; larking around the hedgerows and withybeds is fun for the hounds, but it does have the disadvantage of making them too 'eyesy'. There is nothing wrong with a hound's eyesight, but it is insignificant compared with its nose. If hounds see too many foxes they will start looking for them instead of smelling for them, and that will not make for a good working hound.

My own hunting country is different yet again. In the main it consists of some twenty miles of open, rolling hill. It has roads into it, to isolated farms, but no roads through it. There are few coverts, except at the west end where there are 7,000 acres of forestry. The foxes are bred out on the hill, in old rabbit holes or rock clitters, and there are huge bracken beds which provide great covert for them. Bracken provides a particular problem for hunting. Hounds can hunt through it quite well, when it is green, or when it is dead. When bracken is dying, it stinks to such an extent that it foils hounds completely. Because of this there is often a period, in October when hunting on the hills becomes very difficult, and we always hope that the state of the harvest will allow us to visit the low-ground (inbye) coverts during this period.

There is no harvest to worry about on the hills. As a shepherd friend of mine says, 'the only cereals up here are either in a cornflake packet, or a whisky bottle'. This means that we can start hunting as early in the autumn as we like, or as time and resources allow. You might get away with semi-fit horses for trotting around a covert in an inbye country, but for the hills they have to be galloping fit, right from the start. This point was emphasised, in early September a year or two ago, when

'Ware riot' – the whipper-in

we had a hunt of 23 miles with a 7-mile point (I do not think it can have been a cub). It is not usually logistically possible to have horses fit enough before September; so if we want to start in August, which we do, it means foot and/or motor bikes.

First light is the best time to start, as there is a chance of some overnight drag so that hounds can hunt up to where the cubs are lying. People sometimes ask me whether we hold up. I point out that it is very difficult to hold up 500 acres of bracken, on a 1 in 3 hillside, with a boy, two shepherds and a couple of OAPs. However if any reader would like to come along as

well, we can always give it a try. Once hounds have found, there is very little that the huntsman can do to help, or hinder. I like to find a dry rock, in a good vantage point, sit down, and light my pipe. If into a litter, the hounds are likely to split several ways, and you just have to listen and watch as little parties go rejoicing from bracken bed to bracken bed. You can see the cubs popping to and fro, because cubs tend to keep returning to the same ground the first time that they are hunted. If there is any sort of scent, one lot of hounds will gradually become pre-eminent, and their strengthening cry will draw others to their party. As he tires, the cub will start to turn short in the bracken, the cry will swell, a sudden silence, then the distinctive sound of the worry, and steam rising from the bracken.

If it is a bad scenting morning, it is more likely that a cub will be marked to ground. Hounds marking is a quite distinctive sound, a deep-throated regular 'owf, owf, owf' as they tear and scrabble at the earth. An extraordinary transformation will now take place. Had you looked about you, a minute or two before, you would have seen a panorama of wild rolling hills apparently devoid of human life. Let hounds mark a fox, and, suddenly, everywhere you look there are little hurrying figures festooned with spades and entangled with wildly tugging terriers; tractors will appear; battered pickups and motor cycles will come hurrying from all points of the compass at the prospect of a 'howk'.

Digging

There has been some previous mention of digging, but this seems a good time to consider it in more depth, (and I hope you will excuse the allusion). Digging foxes engenders a certain amount of controversy. Some hunts eschew the practice altogether; others would be hard put to kill any foxes without the help of terrier and spade. As a rule of thumb, the wilder the country the more need there will be for terriers. In most countries there has to be balance. The mounted followers may not take kindly to being expected to sit freezing on their horses

whilst a fox is excavated. They can legitimately point out that is not what they pay their subscriptions for, and can make very sure that higher management are appraised of their complaints. On the other hand, interested local parties such as farmers, shepherds and gamekeepers can be just as forceful in their comments if, every time the local hunt holes a fox, they just ride away and leave him. If I quote: 'you brought the bugger yere; now you dig him out; if you leave that fox you won't come scousing over my land no more', you begin to appreciate the problem.

The answer is that every hunt should have a responsible terrier man, either professional or amateur, who can be left behind in charge of the operations whilst the hunt goes on to find another fox. If the shades of winter night are falling, or it is the end of a cubhunting morning, the situation is different. The master is then duty bound to try and get that fox for his hounds. The huntsman should always want his hounds to get their fox, and should do everything possible to achieve this end. Hounds always know and love a trier, and will knock their guts out for him in return.

Let us return to the earth. Suppose I were to hand the average man a terrier and a spade, and tell him to dig a fox out, he probably wouldn't have the faintest idea of how to go about it; it is skilled work when done well. The first thing to decide is whether the fox is to be bolted and hunted again, or dug out and shot with a humane killer. Rule 18 of the MFHA is quite unequivocal; it states:

Should a fox be run to ground one of the following alternatives must be strictly adhered to:

(a) He should be left where he is.
(b) He should be bolted and given a fair and sporting chance of escape.
(c) If for various reasons it is essential that he be killed, he should be dug up to and immediately destroyed, before being given to the hounds.

The next thing to do is to have the hounds taken away, out of sight and sound. The earth should then be assessed as to soil type, area, and possible depth. Soil type is important. For instance, I am always reluctant to allow a terrier into green sand. This is notoriously unstable stuff and caves in very easily, with dangerous consequences to terriers and diggers. Loam is good digging. Clay is hard graft. On the hills, there is often moorband – hard, gravelly soil down to a layer of hardened sandstone, under which the holes will run; you will have to bar and pick every inch. You may wonder that people will undertake such labour, but the fact is that men who would have to be forced grumbling, at point of rolling pin, into the garden at home, will happily dig for hours in wind, rain and black dark to get a fox. An earth may be a single hole (in which case it usually goes deep), or it may have several 'eyes'. All the holes must be found.

If it is to be a bolting job, all the holes are opened up, the terrier is loosed, and the cast retires out of sight to await developments. Good working terriers come in various shapes, sizes and colours. The one thing they all have in common is immense courage and tenacity. Would you go to ten, or more, feet underground, in total darkness, to face a brave and savage foe who can be up to twice your size? I would not, and for that and many other reasons, working terriers hold a very special place in my affections. Some terriers are so hard that they will fight a fox to the death below ground. These dogs are too hard for normal hunt work, but they are prized for work in the big rock borrans in the fells, where lamb-worrying foxes have to be destroyed at all costs. A good dog should get up to his fox and, standing off, so discomfort him with its baying that the fox will decide to make his excuses and leave. The digging party will watch the bolted fox, and when he has been given sufficient law a cap will go up as signal to the huntsman. A click of the tongue is all that is necessary to release the pent-up hounds, and a wave of lemon, white and brown comes pouring down the hill to pick up the line and go chiming away.

An excavation is a different matter. The first move is to block all the holes except the one that is to be worked on. The terrier is fired in, and everybody waits and listens until distant baying tells that the dog is confronting the fox. In the old days it was thought that the best thing to do was to 'follow on the hole', that is to dig along the line of the hole, following the sound, until you reached the terrier. This could result in some really massive earth-moving operations, such as Messrs Wimpey and Costain would not be ashamed of. It could be immensely time consuming, and could result in the destruction of the earth, which is ecologically undesirable.

These days scientific methods are applied; we have the 'bleeper'. The terrier has a collar which carries a tiny transmitter; the signal is received by a hand-held receiver on the surface. By varying the strength of the bleep it is not only possible to establish the exact position of the terrier, but also how deep it is. Most bleepers have a range of 15 feet. If the dog is deeper than that you will be well advised to abort the mission anyway. The bleeper enables the diggers to 'crown down' on the exact spot where the dog is baying the fox, thus saving a lot of digging and disruption. If you get down 6 of the 7 feet, and the fox moves to another part of the earth, you just have to spit, shrug, and start again. The next pot might be shallower, but I would not bank on it. To use a bleeper accurately requires practice. It is best done at home. Follow the example of a certain noble lord who got his butler to crawl about under the dining-room table with the collar, whilst he practised with the receiver above.

When the diggers get down to the fox, the dog is removed to safety, and the fox is shot. Let this be done by a competent person; a pistol in a confined space is not a thing to be handled lightly. I remember a certain terrier man, on a certain Boxing Day, who had made the season much too festive. This man had a little German automatic which he had liberated from Adolf Hitler. This day a fox was run to ground and dug before a large, enthusiastic holiday crowd. When the moment came to

Tired hounds on their beds after a day's hunting

despatch the fox, it became quickly apparent that all was not well. The first shot killed the terrier, whereupon our hero fell over backwards and raked the surrounding area with a burst of rapid, creating amongst the onlookers a unanimous desire to clasp the muddy field to their collective bosom. He then shot himself in the foot, and the fox bolted over his prostrate wailing form. It was all rather badly done. Badly done is what terrier work should never be. I repeat that it is skilled work, and that skill can only be acquired by experience.

Dates for cubhunting

Cubhunting continues until the opening meet; 1 November is the official start of the foxhunting season, and most packs hold their opening meet on, or soon after, that date. Some packs have even taken to holding their opening meets in the middle of October, on the basis that modern farming pressures mean the season finishing earlier than it used to. I understand the reason-

ing, but do not agree with it. The curtailment of the cubhunting could well have a bad effect on the hounds, with future bad
effects on the sport.

September and October are the main cubhunting months,
and as the country becomes more open, and hounds and horses
become fitter, so the hunting becomes more wide ranging.
There can be very exciting hunting in October, and it is well
worth having your horse fit enough to enjoy it. A word of caution here. A lot of horses break down from being worked too
soon. Some people drag their horses in from the field the week
before the opening meet, and are surprised when they go lame
the day after. There are no short cuts to equine fitness. It is a
minimum of 6 weeks from grazing field to hunting field, including an initial 2 weeks' solid walking. 'No foot, no 'oss'; if
you do not get the legs hard to begin with, then all else is a
waste of time, and money.

Dress
What should you wear? The correct dress is ratcatcher, which
has been detailed in Chapter 5. However, we live in busy
times; most people going cubhunting will be snatching an hour
or two before office or the school run, and so the answer is,
whatever is practical and comfortable. Do not be too
intimidated by the immaculate gleaming figure of old General
Potleigh; he has umpteen grooms and ex-soldier servant,
Launder, to see that he is clean, dry and lightly oiled.

A TYPICAL CUBHUNT

We will run through a typical cubhunting morning, so that you
have some idea of the sights and sounds that you may
encounter. The Blankshire are having their first morning at
Goblin Wood (a deciduous woodland of some 60 acres), at
0600 hours on 32 August. Unless it is very close to your home,
I strongly advise you to box your horse to the meet. Late for
work people, driving half asleep down darkened country lanes,

will not be on the lookout for almost invisible horses. Get everything ready the night before. Lay all your kit out, and check it, so that you can fall into it with your eyes half shut.

If you are fortunate to live close to the kennels, you will be in no doubt that hunting is imminent; hounds will be singing, on and off, throughout the night. I always used to go and tell mine the night before, but they always know anyway; they are fit, keyed up, and ready to go; they sense the beginning of another season, and they celebrate with song. The sound of hounds singing in the kennel, on a fine summer night, is pure magic. I have had people complain to me about the noise, but they are surely dull, soulless creatures. A silent kennel is wrong; hounds sing when they are in good mental and physical shape. A single hound will start, and gradually the chorus will swell, decline, swell again, and gradually subside. There will be a spell of silence, then another performance, to be repeated at intervals throughout the night, until the sound of the huntsman's early morning footstep sets the whole chorus swelling again, fortissimo; they know that they are going to do the thing that they are born for. Our soulless friend will have spent the night with the blankets over his head complaining about 'bloody dogs howling', but there is nothing discordant about the singing; eerie, yes, for perhaps it touches some atavistic disquiet; after all, wolf packs do the same thing. I am not musical, but musical friends tell me that, when hounds sing, the opener sets the key and all the others join in, in that key; just like the Ystradggynlais male voice choir, in fact, so 'there's lovely' I say.

As Goblin Wood is just down the back lane from the kennels, hounds will hack on, and as all your organisation last night means that you are in good time, why not go by the kennels and go down with them? In spite of the early hour, there will be several people assembled in the morning dimpsey, and lights of cars heading down the lane. The chorus in the kennels rises to frenzy as the mounted hunt staff appear from the stables; a wave from the huntsmen; the kennel gate is opened; and the torrent pours out, baying and leaping about the huntsman's

horse. Old Moses, the cob, is on his tenth cubhunting; he stands like a rock, taking no notice of hounds in and out of his legs. May your horse be as steady; if he is not, for the sake of all, keep him well out of the way. There is no good moment to kick a hound, but this is definitely a worse one. The huntsman will give hounds time to settle, and empty, then a little whistle, and off they go – a living tide of waving sterns and grinning faces, duochrome, in the dusk.

In the field by the covert there will be a pause. The hounds will be gathered round the huntsman, quivering with tension. The master will be sending people to strategic points around the covert, with instructions to 'give him a turn if you can'. There are places where a fox will be more likely to break than others; foxes make maximum use of dead ground so that hedgebacks, ditches and dips in the ground are all likely points of departure. It will probably be best if you attach yourself to an experienced follower, who will be able to explain the proceedings to you. After you have taken up your position, there will be a few moments of silence; fill your lungs with autumn air, and explore the smells of an English, autumn, dawn.

As soon as the master considers that there has been time enough for people to get into position, he will give the huntsman the nod. The huntsman will take his hounds quietly to the covertside; 'Leu in, my dears'. The old hounds will be through the fence in a flash. The young hounds will be confused, and will follow the huntsman as he slips through the wicket into the covert. The first sound you will hear will be the huntsman's voice, drawing. Some huntsmen make too much noise, some too little; no two huntsman sound exactly the same. It is hardly possible to reproduce many hunting noises on paper, or reduce them to words, but there are some excellent records on the market, and you would be well advised to invest in one; it will give you some idea of what to expect. All hunting noises should have a purpose; that of informing hounds, and followers, what is happening. The long drawn out drawing noise also encourages the hounds to go deep into the

The Vale of Clettwr hounds beginning to draw a covert in Wales

thickets, whilst still being in touch with their huntsman. Hounds hate being left behind. If they cannot hear their huntsman, they will be very loathe to stray far from him. You hear people say that such a pack draws well, and such a pack draws badly; all hounds have the capacity to draw well, it is the huntsman's fault if they do not.

The huntsman will move slowly along the ride, the puppies trailing after him. The old hounds will all be out of sight, their sensitive noses exploring, and analysing, every tantalising whiff that comes their way. Old Senator appears, nose wiffling, stern thrashing from side to side; he shoots across the ride. The huntsman pauses, and sits quietly; Senator is truth on four legs. Seconds later, the old dog's hoarse roar comes from the bushes: 'Fox! Fox! Fox!' he proclaims, and the first morning of a new season is under way.

Once the litter is roused, there will soon be several lots of hounds in operation, each hunting their own fox. The experienced huntsman will now stay very quiet; no vocal participation is required from him; he can just trot about the rides, listening and observing. The thrilling cry of their seniors will start to infect the youngsters, and as the morning wears on the number of puppies following the huntsman will decrease, as more and more of them join in.

Outside the covert, you will be standing quietly. If the cry of the hounds does not raise a little prickle around the back of your neck, it is possible that you might be better off in bed. There is a sudden flicker of movement at the edge of the covert and a flash of red; there he is, a well-grown cub, picking his way quietly along the fence. Your companion starts to tap his stick on his boot: 'Hi Charlie, Charlie'; the cub looks up, startled, turns like a flash, and disappears into the covert. The companion raises his voice, and bellows 'Tally-ho bike', which tells the huntsman that a fox has gone back into the covert.

Further round the covert, a chorus of yells announces the sighting, and departure, of a fox. Your morning is enlivened by the sight of two 17-stone countrymen on high-speed collision course. The old vixen is not having any, and she is away and gone, leaving a heaving mass of impacted agricultural craftsman on the ground. It has to be said that hunting does tend to get people over excited, on occasion; after all it is supposed to be exciting.

The sharpness of the action will depend, as everything does in hunting, on the scent. Foxes live by scent, and understand it thoroughly. If there is a good scent, and hounds can really run in the covert, the foxes will be looking for off. On a bad scenting morning, the foxes will just dawdle about in the covert, and will hardly bother to show themselves. If the autumn is truly one of 'mists and mellow fruitfulness', the best of the scent will be in the first hour or so of early morning, while the dew is still on the ground. As the day gets warmer, and drier, and as the covert gets more foiled, the work for the hounds gets harder. I

Cubhunting: followers lining a covert

have known mornings when hounds ran with such dash and
cry that the problem was in getting them to come away from
the covert before they scrunched up the whole litter of cubs;
but that sort of morning is rare. On a normal cubhunting, the
scent starts to deteriorate just as hounds and foxes are getting
tired. It is then that, as was mentioned earlier, the huntsman
should persuade his tired, thirsty hounds that if they force their
way through the thorns just once more they will catch their
fox; and very often that is when they do.

Our morning is a typical autumn morning. Hounds are running with a great cry for this first cool hour. A small lot are
hunting steadily in the covert near you and, suddenly, there he
is, a big strong cub, coming straight towards you. Your companion is alert: 'He looks a good 'un. Let er go, eh?'; the cub
slides past you. Some hounds come out of covert on the line. A
whipper-in appears apparently out of the ground, and on being
told that the fox has gone, stops the hounds, quietly, and urges
them on to the swelling cry of those still running in the covert.

There is a new intensity in the sound, an increasing excitement. The hunted fox is running short, turning sharply in the thick undergrowth, trying to make hounds overrun the line; but the scent is good, and the hounds match him, turn for turn. The cry swells again, then a sudden silence, and, from the thicket, the unmistakable, thick growling sound of the kill.

'They've got him', there is an excited rush from around the covert, and from the inner thickness the huntsman's shrill 'Who whoop'. He appears, struggling through the clinging undergrowth, carrying the limp corpse above his head, the old hounds leaping and baying around him, the puppies joining in the excitement, although they are still not too sure what it is all about. Once clear of the covert, the huntsman allows hounds to 'break up' their fox, encouraging them with horn and voice; the bolder puppies take a tentative grab or two; their time will come. A word of warning: should you ever find yourself alone with hounds when they catch a fox, you would be very ill-advised to try to remove the corpse; it could end in tears.

The morning is getting warmer. Gathered intelligence suggests that at least four foxes have gone away, but it is thought that there is at least one still in the covert. The master and the huntsman confer, and decide to have 'one more cut'. Hounds are taken back to the covert. For a long time there is no sound except for the huntsman's voice, encouraging the hounds. The heat is increasing now, the scent in the already foiled covert waning all the time; people start to look at their watches, and think about the work that has to be done. It seems more and more likely that all the foxes have gone.

In the middle of the covert, there is a section where thorns and small bushes have been laid, cut half through, and laid over, so that they go on growing horizontally; this provides snug, safe lying for foxes. Only hounds will venture into such a tangled mass, and the huntsman is patiently encouraging his to face the thorns once more. From the middle of the thick comes a whimper, then quiet; the huntsman waits; another whimper, then a full-throated roar. 'Leu at him', shouts the huntsman,

and the cry swells again. But the scent has gone now, and the cub is just creeping about in the thick. Hounds can only speak here and there as they puzzle out the failing line; it is patience and perseverance now with the real heat of the day beginning. There is a long spell of silence. The huntsman looks at his watch, and maybe thinks of the breakfast that he has not yet had. Then from the edge of the covert there is the unmistakable sound of old Statesman marking. The cub has crept into a field drain, and there is a good chance of finishing the morning on the right note.

HAREHUNTING

Harehunting also starts in autumn, following the harvest. August and September meets tend to be in the early morning, for the same reasons as in cubhunting. The early hunting is not conducted on vastly different lines to harehunting proper. There is no holding up, however, harehunting being a sport of the open country; there is not the pressure to kill the hare as there is with the fox; nor is there a mounted field to upset the young hounds. For these reasons, harehunters tend to start their season proper earlier than foxhunters, opening meets often being held in October, or even September. Even so, a wise master will allow due time to get his young hounds settled, and hunting, before he lets the general public join in.

There is no doubt in my mind that beagles are much easier to handle than foxhounds; they have a more equable temperament, suffer fools to a greater extent, and come to their work quicker. The fact that the huntsman is limited by his own foot-power means that most beagles suffer less interference than most foxhounds; a fact which is greatly in their favour. If more packs of foxhounds were hunted on foot, there would be many better packs of foxhounds; but fewer followers to pay for them. There is a saying in the sheepdog world that 'there are no bad dogs; only bad handlers'; every huntsman of every pack of hounds should have that painted on his shaving mirror.

8
Winter Hunting

THE OPENING MEET

The 'opening meet': now there is an evocative phrase. If you do not have the odd raw nerve-end before your first opening meet, you will hardly be human, and the same feeling should reappear every year. It is a grand occasion; a time for parade-ground turnout, formal manners, overfresh horses, unfit people – the start of another season, and all the excitement and glorious uncertainty that that betokens. I have carried the horn at twenty-one opening meets, and whilst I was never in a greater funk than I was on the first occasion, my terror was in no way diminished on the twenty-first.

The foxhunting season opens, officially, on 1 November, as your diary should tell you if it is the better sort of diary (the great Mr Letts of Letts' diaries is a master of hounds). Most hunts hold their opening meet on, or close to, the first; the first Saturday in November being the most general date.

The venue for the opening meets tends to be established by tradition, which tends to create logistical problems for the management. For instance, the Blankshire have held their

opening meet at the Magpie and Stump since before anyone can remember. The Magpie and Stump currently has a motorway on two sides, a conurbation on the third, whilst the fourth, which provides the only outlet to open country, is ruled by a vulpicidal shooting syndicate, who always arrange to shoot on the day of the opening meet. If you think that this will mean problems for the master, and precious little chance of sport, you will be absolutely right. However, if you want to find out what it feels like when the sky falls on your head, just suggest changing the opening meet.

The master

Let us look at the opening meet through the eyes of some of the dramatis personae. First, the master; his problems will be greatly increased with the start of the season proper. He can no longer skulk about as he has been doing for the last two months, doing his own thing; he is now expected to start earning the honour of being allowed to subsidise other peoples' pleasure, by producing some sport for them. In most hunting countries, in the 1980s, laying on a day's hunting can be something of an administrative nightmare. A pack of hounds can cover a great area in the course of a day, and it is the master's job to see that the path is broad and smooth before them.

At one time the procedure was fairly simple; the master rang up a couple of landowners, whose broad acres would encompass the day's sport, and the thing was done. If the master felt particularly modern, and democratic, he might even go so far as to put the meets in the local paper; otherwise it was left to the four-ale-bar intelligence system, which should never be underrated. Things are not so simple today; the big estates have gone, or have shrunk. The majority of farmers are owner-occupiers, with swingeing overdrafts and a healthy sense of their own independence, and importance. I remember the shock of an old MFH, following the dissolution of a famous sporting estate, on having a gate slammed in his face with the words 'Lord X is dead now, Sir'; it was a sharp, but salutary lesson.

The Duke of Beaufort's Hunt moving off from an opening meet at Badminton House

As has been stated before, hunting continues by goodwill, and the efficient management of the hunting day is one of the ways that goodwill is maintained. Different countries require different methods. In some intensively farmed areas, it is the custom for every farm that is likely to be involved in a particular day's hunting to be visited by a hunt official beforehand. This can mean contacting thirty farmers, and noting their particular requirements and worries, which will vary with the time of year – oil seed rape and in-calf heifers in autumn, heavy ewes in spring, and grass seeds all the time. Many farmers are keen sportsmen, even if they do not hunt themselves; what a pleasure it is to be told 'come when you like, and go where you like'. Some farmers just do not want to know; usually because they have suffered through someone's thoughtless behaviour

in the past. Sometimes confidence can be restored. A certain man, who was not at all keen on the hounds, to put it mildly, fell in with a good hunt one day whilst out in his Land Rover; he was infected by the excitement, and is now one of the keenest men to hounds in the realm.

Very few farmers are opposed to hunting on ethical grounds; their objections tend to be practical or political. The vast majority occupy the middle ground; they are not especially keen on hunting themselves, although a child, or wife, may well hunt, but they like to see the hounds about; they like to have a fox killed; they may go out in the van for an hour, for a bit of crack with their friends; their neighbour, who is so helpful with machinery, may be a keen hunting man. This majority regards hunting as part of the rural life, and as long as they, personally, suffer no harm from it, they are quite happy to put up with it, join in the social activities, and shrug off the occasional minor irritation. It is the avoidance of these irritations that makes some sort of warning system necessary. It is usually visits, post cards, telephone calls, or variations and combinations of the three. The information gleaned is then collated by the master, who then has to plan his day, and the coverts that he is going to draw, on the basis of the received intelligence.

Farmers are often the least of the master's worries; shooting can be much more of a problem. In the days of the great estates, the shooting was the personal sport of the proprietor. He had broad acres to conduct his shoot in, and no one to please but himself. Even if he did not hunt, the landowner would normally regard it as his duty, as a gentleman and sportsman, to support the hunt, and to keep foxes as well as pheasants. Times have changed. Everybody wants to shoot, and the pressure on available land is acute. People are paying stupid prices to rent the shooting on almost any bit of land, however unsuitable it may be. This means that the master, instead of having, perhaps, half a dozen large, fairly relaxed shoots to deal with, is confronted with a writhing mass of neurotic syndicate shoots, many of whom are trying to extract a quart out of a very highly

Farmer

priced pint pot. I know of a hunting country that has 137 syndicate shoots within its bounds.

It would be nonsense to say that this situation does not present problems. Many of the syndicate members are not local people, indeed not country people; they have no stake in local life; they merely want to roll up; wear amazing suits; shoot as many soft birds as possible; have a good lunch; and get back to town in time for the Rotary Club's Cheese Dip and Glühwein Fest. They are not interested in the local hunt, and they leave everything to their keeper. The sort of man who gets employed by this sort of shoot can be either a reject from a good set up, or an ill-trained vermin catcher, who gets to call himself gamekeeper even if no one else allows him that dignity. Whatever, this unfortunate man is under great pressure; he is the one

who has to convert the sow's ear of a shoot into the silk purse that his employers desire. He has problems, and he does not want the hunt adding to them, especially during the key months of November and December, and especially on Saturdays; he has poisoned all the foxes anyway. It will not take too much imagination to realise that your hunting days take a bit more organisation than you dreamed of.

The modern master will have other factors to consider, when making his dispositions: high speed trains, motorways, and the fact that for instance Steeple Sinderby (pop 250), through the outskirts of which the Skinner's Gorse foxes traditionally run, has overnight become an Urban Resettlement Area for 15,000 people, to whom hunting will be an experience outside the scope of what they have come to regard as normal life. You may now begin to understand why masters sometimes seem somewhat preoccupied, and why their fuses may burn short, on occasion. In fact you may wonder how they ever manage to smile at all; some of them never do.

If the master hunts his hounds as well, he is shouldering a double burden, and you could well be justified in wondering why he should wish to. The answer is fairly simple: to hunt a good pack of hounds, well, is one of the most difficult, most fascinating, most exciting; most physically and mentally, demanding things a man can aspire to do. A good day puts you on a high, above the cloud ceiling, a bad day reduces you to the bottom of the pit of misery; perhaps it is one of the great challenges available to a man today. I am quite certain that no one who has tasted the fairy sweetness of hunting a pack of hounds, will ever find his life quite the same again; it is to achieve this that many men seek, and suffer, all the myriad problems and worries that the mastership of a pack will inevitably bring.

The huntsman
The huntsman, be he master or man, has his own set of problems and worries, once the start of hunting proper begins. The

The MFH

man who is not nervous is unlikely to be a successful huntsman. Hunting a pack of hounds requires a bit of fire and dash. They say that you can tell a huntsman by his hounds; if the hounds are flat and lack lustre, you can be certain that the huntsman is calm to the point of boredom. I remember a certain lady talking about a certain huntsman; she said, 'You see him going to the first covert; he is grinding his teeth, and all his hounds are trotting around him all grinding their teeth and thinking "Gnash, gnash; fox, fox"; and you know that if there is a fox in the covert, he better go, and quick too.' That is the sort of frame of mind a huntsman should be in. The hounds will always know exactly his mood, and will reflect it. If they do not, it means that they have no empathy with the man, and he would be better employed running ICI or a whelk stall.

The hunting of a pack of hounds is a very demanding task physically. The huntsman has to go all day, and every hunting day; he may well be in the saddle for seven or eight hours; he cannot just pack up and go home because he has a wet bottom, or because he wants to watch the rugger on the telly. He requires a cast-iron constitution. He also requires a resolute mind. The mental strain of hunting hounds is even greater than the physical. From the time he leaves the meet, until the moment he blows for home, the huntsman's job requires total concentration. His mind is working like a sort of computer, into which a continuous stream of data is being fed, and there processed. He will watch, and listen, to his hounds all the time. Which hound spoke first in the covert? Why have the old hounds dropped back from the lead, have they changed foxes? If the hounds divide, which lot is right? Have hounds driven over the line and, if so, how far? he will watch for changes in wind and weather as carefully as any sailor; for these will affect the scenting conditions and the way he handles the hounds. He will watch out for all problems ahead: a big flock of sheep, an extensive block of plough ground, that single motor car on a distant road that just might have turned the fox. This is just a fraction of the continuous stream of data that the huntsman has

to take in, process, and sometimes base instant decisions on —
decisions which may mean the difference between success or
failure for the hounds; and between you having a memorable
hunt or going home wishing that you had watched the rugger
after all. On top of all this, the huntsman has to remember that
he is an entertainer; that it is part of his job to make the day enjoyable. He somehow has to make time to be pleasant, to greet
all men, and even to manage the occasional rough jest, if he be
so blessed. If he has the occasional lapse from grace, you must
put it in the context of the strain the man is under.

There is no doubt that many huntsmen are unable to cope.
Some fail through lack of skill, but some very able men have
failed through an inability to cope with the stress. There were
moments when my career hiccuped badly. I was always fortunate in that there was always some senior, respected foxhunter
who took the trouble to pick me up, kick my bum, and set me
back on the path. Other men have not been so lucky, and have
sought to relieve their pressures by methods generally
unacceptable to hunt committees, and their careers have floun-
dered. It is a hard row to hoe.

The whole emphasis of the huntsman's job changes with the
opening meet. Throughout cubhunting, he has had to worry
about nothing but his hounds, and getting them settled and
hunting in proper style. Once the opening meet and hunting
proper has come, his duty, and that of his hounds, is to provide
the goods for the paying customers.

Getting to the meet

Now that we have discussed the two main members of the cast,
and explained the reasons for them being just a little on edge at
the opening meet, let us see about getting you there.

I will not bang on about the need for having your horse fit.
You may think it would be boring and unnecessary. However
you will be amazed how many people think it quite all right to
get their pig-fat, lard-soft horse in from the field at the end of
October, with a view to hunting it at the opening meet. They

are then amazed, in their turn, when their horse spends most of the season swelling the current account of the local veterinary practice. Unless the sport with your chosen pack is quite unusually bad, you just will not get away with it.

So your horse is hard fit; now it will need to be clipped. If you keep your horse at livery, all that should be taken care of (if they charge you extra for clipping, you are being stitched up). You may wish to do your own clipping; my advice is to leave it alone and get in an expert. There are people in every country who will clip horses for a greater, or lesser, fee; take local advice. Clipping is one of those things that look dead easy when you see an expert doing them and the result is superb. You will find that it is not easy to do well, and a badly clipped horse will never look like anything except a badly clipped horse.

You will have checked all your tack very, very thoroughly, and cleaned it ditto; anything that looks the slightest bit doubtful, you should take to the saddler's. Remember: your neck just may depend on that little strap, which you thought just might do. I wonder if you had your saddle fitted by the saddler; it is very important that the saddle fits both you and the horse. A good saddle is a very good investment.

To plait, or not to plait, the mane is a vexed question. All grooms, and horsy ladies, are compulsive plaiters, and the thought of the opening meet brings out the worst in them. Plaiting is time consuming, and difficult. I have always reckoned that a well-bred horse needs no plaiting, whilst it makes common horses look even worse. This theory always produces shrieks of anguish from the stables. My advice is to have your horse's mane hogged (crew cut), then no one has any excuse for wasting time over it.

A coloured browband on a hunter is definitely Charlie. I know that certain noble packs have browbands in the family livery colours; when you are ennobled, and have a family livery, you will get away with it too; not until then. I would thoroughly recommend having a breastplate on your horse; they are smart, practical, and give you a crafty handhold when

'No 1 dress is the order of the day . . .'

jumping. It is impossible to check the tension of your girth too often.

Now we must get you dressed. We know what you are going to wear from Chapter 5, and I very much hope that you have managed to get it all in time. If you are 'off the peg', there should not be too much of a problem. However 'bespoke' is another story. All good tailors take their time, and this is especially so with breeches, the cutting of which is a particular skill. Very few tailors have their own breeches' cutter any more, and the work is farmed out to a few specialists who frankly get overwhelmed. It is not a bit of good you breezing into the tailor at the end of September and demanding full fig in time for the opening meet; there will likely be wailing and gnashing of teeth. Order all your stuff no later than the end of June, and even that is cutting it fine.

This principle of never being in a bad hurry, is one that applies right through hunting, and never more so than on a hunting morning. Get everything ready the day before. For the opening meet, and all subsequent meets, No 1 dress is the order

of the day; and you want to be as clean, and tidy, and highly polished, as you know how to be. No one will mind if your clothes are old, but a lot of people will mind if they are dirty; and so should you. You cannot get everything up to scratch on the morning of the opening meet; get everything clean and polished before, and have it laid out ready to climb into on the morning. Work out how much time you are going to need to get all your chores done, and to get yourself to the meet in good time, then add at least an hour; all households are chaotic on hunting mornings.

Senior hunting people will tell you that it is a shame that it is no longer practical to hack on to the meet in most countries; there is some justification for this statement. Hacking would give both you, and your horse, time to settle down and get tuned in to the day; you would both arrive at the meet in a better frame of mind. Hacking also gives you a chance to have a crack with those whom you meet on the road; this form of contact should not be underestimated in the continuous process of maintaining relations between those who hunt, and those whose basic goodwill will help hunting to continue and always thank cars that slow down for you, thereby encouraging them to do so again.

What dear old Major Luce-Rayne does not say much about are the joys of hacking home – the blackbirds chinking in the bushes, and the lights coming on in the vale below as you breast the final hill. Therefore, let me suggest the reverse side of the disc: dusk coming on; incipient influenza; horse not quite sound; the first snow flakes falling; and fifteen chilling, cramping, bone weary miles between you and home. With modern traffic conditions it is simply foolish to consider riding home in the dark. I have not considered it for years. I can remember stumbling through the dark and wet for four hours or more, and falling asleep in the saddle on occasion; I do not recommend it. It is one of the good moments of the day when, having inserted myself into a large overcoat, and a warm lorry cab, I get the thermos flask out and relive the high spots of the day.

The Bramham Moor foxhounds unboxing

We have not touched on horse transport: how you manage it will depend on circumstances, and pocket. The trailer/car/ Land Rover is certainly the most generally used form, but whatever your transport is, the main thing is to park it sensibly. Wherever possible park off the road, and out of the way. Please *do not* park in gateways, or across other peoples' driveways: imagine how you would feel if you could not get to the shops because some prune had parked a car, and trailer, bang across your entrance: do as you would be done by. By the same token, if someone has chosen to manicure a stretch of roadside, please think how he is going to feel if your rig is sunk to the axles in it. Many people are incapable of reversing a trailer: if you too are a member of this select band, you would be well advised to plan your parking for each meet so that you can drive away, at the end of the day, without the entire local-

ity being conscripted to un-muddle you. Try to park well away from the meet, and hack on the last half mile or so; this will get you, and your horse, settled. Neither of you wants to arrive foaming, mentally and physically.

There is always a big turn out of horse, and foot, at the opening meet. You will probably see the hunt staff, and the hounds, tucked up in some secure corner. This is not because they are feeling unsociable, but because they are terrified of any of the hounds being awarded a penalty kick by any one of the large number of overcorned, overwrought horses that are milling about. However, it is considered correct to say 'good morning' to the master; if you are male, you should also raise your hat, but if you feel diffident about this he will probably not worry about it too much. You should make your number with the Hon Secretary; you should not go and hide behind the church, in hope of avoiding the payment of your just dues, nor should he be such a clown as to allow you to get away with it.

Have a drink, at the meet; indeed, have two, if you wish; it is an enjoyable social occasion. However if you find it necessary to get legless at the meet, you should ask yourself whether you may be wasting your time bothering about the hunting at all. To the best of my knowledge and belief you can be arrested for being drunk in charge of a horse, under an Act of 1895; I understand the maximum fine to be 30 shillings.

The hunt is on

The great moment is at hand, and hounds are sweeping away up the road. The field master is the person you must follow. Every now and again the column will grind to a halt; this is because a hound has stopped to 'empty'. No one should attempt to ride past it; it should be allowed to pursue its evacuation in total peace, and security.

Soon you turn off the road through a gateway. Do not bump the horses in front of you; it is ill-mannered, and dangerous. Most field masters like to group their charges in a spot where they can keep a beady eye on them, and prevent some of the

sneakier citizens from sidling off on their own. You will see a select few being despatched; these are the 'points', experienced sportsmen who will take up key positions around the covert, and watch, and wait, until one of them marks the departure of the fox with that most thrilling of hunting sounds (when well done) – the 'View Holloa (pronounced holler)'. If you should get sent on point, at some stage, remember this: always stand close to the covert, watch the dead ground, and when a fox does slip away, bite your lip and count thirty before you holloa. To holloa too soon, turn the fox back, and have the entire hunt hanging on your explanation, can be a humiliating experience.

In a well-run hunt, the points should be in position before the rest of the field arrive at the covert (pronounced cover) side, so that no time is wasted. The huntsman will take his hounds to the covert side, and pause; a well-mannered pack of hounds should pause as well, albeit straining with impatience. A quiet 'leu in there', and they will disappear into the covert.

If the whole country has been properly covered during the cubhunting, the litters should have been well dispersed, and the foxes wary, and ready to run. The first fox to go away from a covert is, usually, the boldest, and the best; this is the one that the huntsman will want to be on, but this is not always a simple operation. If it is a good scenting day (scent is such a complex subject that it is dealt with separately, later), and the foxes are wild, a fox may be away before hounds even get to the covert, and the huntsman can scoot round to the holloa, lay hounds on the line, and everything is hop, ding away pop. More usually the covert will have to be drawn, and the field will have to preserve itself in varying degrees of patience and barely suppressed nervous prostration. How well you survive this nerve-jangling time will depend on your own system; time alone will tell.

You will now hear the sound of the huntsman drawing, which will be much as you heard during cubhunting. The way the huntsman uses his horn and voice for this operation will depend somewhat on circumstances, and his evaluation of the

Drawn blank

prevailing conditions. As a general rule, the more noise he makes, the further his hounds will spread. So, if the covert is a small one with a large population of foxes, he will make little noise because he wants his hounds to stay handy by, closely grouped, so that they are likely to get together on one fox. He does not want them hunting in three, or four different lots, on this occasion. On the other hand, if he is drawing a large covert, which may well have only one fox in it, he will not want to miss that fox; so he will use plenty of voice, both to encourage his hounds to spread and the fox to get on his feet.

The huntsman's voice grows fainter as he gets further away. Your companions start to mutter 'not at home'. There is no such thing as a 'sure find', although you will hear people talk about them; the fox is a wild animal, he lies where he wants to,

and does not take the desires of the local hunt into consideration when choosing his bedroom. From the other end of the
covert, comes the sound of the horn: a series of long, mourn-
ful, drawn out notes. This is the 'drawn blank'. At the same
time you will hear the whipper-in's voice, 'Cope, cope cope,
come along, cope, cope'; long and drawn out, again.

You bump down the side of the covert to where the staff are
sitting with the hounds. The whipper-in is standing in his stir-
rups, surveying the assembled hounds with furrowed brow; he
sits down, 'all on, Sir', he says to the huntsman. This means all
present and correct; yes, he was actually counting that seeth-
ing, jumbled mass. You might think you could never manage
that, but you could with lots of practice, and plenty of
bollockings if you got it wrong.

On to the next covert; a man in a tattered brown smock and
clarty boots holds a gate open for you all to pass through. As a
matter of course, everyone thanks him, and wishes him a good
day; just as well, for he is the owner-occupier of the 400 acres
on which you are about to squander.

The field forms up outside the next covert, the hounds are
put in, and there is the sound of the huntsman drawing. Then
there is a whimper, then another one, then a deep strangled
roar: 'Hike to Statesman; hike, hike, hike!' It is sharp staccato
from the huntsman, now, and the cry doubles, trebles and
swells. It is now the huntsman's earnest desire to keep all his
hounds together, hunting the one fox, and to persuade that fox
to vacate the premises as quickly as possible. To achieve both
these ends, he makes judicious use of noise; but a sharp, ur-
gent, come my lads there's a fox afoot, sort of noise. He will
ride as close to his lead hounds as the covert permits, and cheer
them on. Different huntsman have different cheers, but the
type of noise should be unmistakable; he will also use his horn
in a short series of short sharp notes known as 'doubling'. The
purpose is to keep the tail hounds joined up to the leaders, and
to convey a sense of urgency to the fox. From the far side of the
covert comes a long drawn out screech; it is the holloa.

The whipper-in – the holloa!

All around you, your companions will have been making their last minute cock-pit checks; check your girth one last time, and get your hat well rammed down. 'Steady the Buffs', says the field master, or 'Hold hard, you bloody shower', according to his own particular temperament and liver status. There is a barely controlled stampede down the covert side, with some naked nerve-ends well displayed, and through a gate. 'Hold hard! Hold hard! Give hounds a chance', is the cry. Further down the field a man is standing with his cap in the air, his horse facing away from the covert; he is the man who holloaed. He is silent now; hounds are coming his way, and any further noise from him would be a distraction not a help. The cry swells in the covert, and the first hounds come tumbling out over the fence and seize the line in the open field. The

huntsman crams through the wicket, sizes up the situation, and blows the 'gone away'.

To describe the gone away as a series of short and long notes blown urgently, is no description at all. Blown by an artist, it will make your back hairs stand up; blown badly, it will give you indigestion. It is only sounded at this supreme moment when hounds are going away on their fox. A well-handled pack of hounds, who trust their huntsman, would fly to it through the hob of Hades. It will make the most sedate hunter hump his back a little.

The whipper-in comes galloping round the covert side: he is also contributing to the general haroosh: 'Forrard away, forrard away, forrard away', he shouts; this again is only used for this particular occasion. As a general principle, there cannot be too much *good* noise for the going away. The great sin is to sneak away with a fox, leaving some hounds in the covert, and the field gossiping on the other side.

Hounds should be counted away from the covert. If the whipper-in is there and gets the 'make' (ie all on), he will shout, 'Cop forrard, Sir' to the huntsman. If the huntsman makes them, he will blow three long notes on the horn to inform the whipper-in. The horn can then be returned to its case on the saddle, and the huntsman can concentrate on riding to his hounds.

It is not always this simple to get hounds away on their fox. Suppose a fox goes away, but hounds are hunting another, in the covert; or hounds divide and run in two, or three, lots. Suppose the fox refuses to leave and appears quite happy to spend the next two hours running in ever decreasing circles in the covert, to the ever increasing fury of the paying customers who are shivering outside. Suppose the fox goes one field, meets the massed ranks of the car followers, and goes straight back to the covert. All these, and many other supposes, are little teasers which the huntsman has to resolve. Each teaser has several different options which will vary according to the ability of the huntsman, the efficiency of the hounds, the weather,

the scent, and, very likely, the Dow Jones Index. The point is that we are looking at highly technical situations, which huntsmen love to talk about, but which most people who enjoy their hunting are quite ignorant of. If you do want to discuss them, you should, as already indicated, take a spare night, a spare bottle of whisky, and some spare huntsmen; you will get all technicalities that you crave.

Let us return to your particular situation. Hounds are away from the covert, and settled on the line. The huntsman has stuck his horn in its case. All around you people are getting their excited horses collected, and again ramming their hats down. This is your last chance to see that everything is tight and comfortable. The field master moves to a trot, still invoking steadiness amongst his flock. When he considers that the hounds have enough room, he will cry 'Follow me' or 'Help yourselves'; whichever the circumstances make most appropriate. The chances are that your headlong career across the first field will end in a queue for a hunt jump. Do not barge, or jump the queue; wait your turn. If your horse will not queue, you would be well advised to send him where his talents will be put to better use; he will be a misery, and a danger, to you and others. Do not jump too close to the horse in front of you; no one likes being jumped on.

If you are in a 'help yourself' sort of country, pick your place in the fence, and go for it. If you wish to ride in the first flight, then you must harden your heart and not chicken out at the last moment. Do not aim for that weak looking place; most bad falls happen just there. Aim for the blackest and thickest part of the fence; if your horse is a jumper, he will take more care of himself, and of you, over a solid looking obstacle. If your ambitions do not run to the first flight, find yourself a pilot who suits your temperament. For instance, dear old Colonel Potleigh, on the redoubtable Moses, is guaranteed to take the stuffing out of any fence. The fact that he is known as 'Pickfords', by the hunt fencing team, should give you great confidence. He always had a devoted band of followers, who

are guaranteed to improve on his initial handiwork.

Let us assume that you are a riding person, in a riding country; your horse is going well; you are taking the obstacles as they come; and it is just possible that you are having the great thrill of your life. There is the surge of a galloping horse, the wind whipping in your face and, all the time, the cry of the hounds floating back to you and urging you on, on, on. If this is your experience, probably your life will never be quite the same again; you will be hooked.

The cry has stopped: there is a 'check'. It is to be hoped that you have had at least half an eye on what is going on around you. If your have been watching the hounds, you will have seen them check in their onward career. There is, as British Telecom are very wont to say, a fault on the line. If the scent is really good, and hounds have got away well with their fox, a fox will do well to stand up for twenty minutes in front of a good pack of hounds. This is called a 'killing scent' is pretty rare, and more likely to happen in the evening than the morning. On an average sort of day, in average sort of country, you will be lucky if hounds run for more than ten minutes without a check. Remember that the fox is the only one who knows where he is going, and the scent that he leaves is the only way of following him. A check occurs when hounds lose that scent, which can happen for a variety of reasons: stock can foil the line, the line can just evaporate, or be blown away; the fox may turn, and hounds may overshoot the line; there may be fresh ploughing, newly spread slurry, 127 cars spread out along the road ahead; the reasons for a check stretch into infinity. Sufficient for you to notice that there is a check, and to react accordingly. What you must do is stop (trying not to cannon into the rear echelon of the field master, who should be in front of you holding up his hand), stand still, and keep quiet. This is also what the huntsman should be doing. If he starts galloping about as soon as hounds check, he is what is known as a 'quick huntsman'; this means he loses foxes quickly.

The huntsman should stand well away from his hounds, and

let them make their own 'cast' first. Casting is what hounds do when seeking to regain the line. Nothing should be done to spoil their concentration, and that includes excited chattering by you, which should earn you rebuke. A good pack of hounds will cast themselves at a hand gallop, first to one side then the other. Nine times out of ten, they will put themselves right and go chiming away; on the tenth occasion, the huntsman will have to start earning his money, and take a hand. All the time he is standing at the check it is to be hoped that his mind is not in neutral; it should be computing. All the relevant data should be feeding into his brain – weather conditions, wind direction, type of ground, likely run of fox, what might have caused him to turn, and exactly what his hounds are doing. On the basis of all this, he will have to decide how to make his cast, should it become necessary. When to cast, and how to do it successfully, is what separates a great huntsman from the also rans.

Just suppose that you see the hunted fox: what should you do about it? It all depends; firstly, are you certain that it is the hunted fox? A very tired, dirty fox is pretty unmistakable, but an untired run fox requires a bit of experience to spot, which you can only get by experience. Many people will say it must be the hunted fox because it has its mouth open, but no fox moves without its mouth open; watch your own dog. Only a very tired fox, close to the end, may have his mouth shut; very few people get to see this.

If you see a fox, and hounds are running, put your cap up and say nothing. If they are hunting your fox, you will soon find out; if they are not, you have still done the right thing. If hounds are checked, and you are *certain* that the fox you have seen is the run fox, you may put your cap up and holloa. A caveat here; that is a general rule. Individual huntsmen and masters have their own ideas, some do not allow holloaing at all; you should find out what local customs prevail. If you are not sure what you have seen, if you are too diffident to holloa, or if you are uncertain in any way, go quietly, without noise or fuss, and quickly tell somebody in authority what you have

seen. This is always the right thing to do.

Once hounds have hit off the line, and are away again, you too can be under way. Remember that it is not always possible for the field to follow wherever the hounds go, for reasons that have already been discussed. In the heat of the moment, with an inviting bit of country before you, common sense may temporarily evaporate. Do heed the field master, and other hunt officials. No one is going to turn away from hounds, unless there is a compelling reason for so doing. In hill country, it is especially important to follow local knowledge; if you bore on regardless, and find yourself up to the axles in a morass with only some speculative looking carrion crows to appeal to, you will only have yourself to blame.

All hunts come to an end. Hounds will eventually either catch their fox, mark it to ground, or run out of scent. Many people hunt all their lives and never actually see a fox caught by hounds. In practice the end often comes in a hedgerow, or a covert. You will arrive, muddy, breathless, and very likely sweating, in a field, in the corner of which there is a struggling mass of tearing, tugging hounds. I would stress, once again, that the fox is not being 'torn to pieces alive', whatever the tabloid press may say. The fox died in an instant, and the excited hounds are eating the corpse, as is their right and their bounden duty; they are 'breaking up' their fox.

Breaking up is a man-induced proceeding: if you hunt with the fell packs, which are seldom attended at the kill, you will see that they seldom break up their foxes; they kill them, tug them about a bit, roll on the carcass, and then leave it. Hounds are encouraged to break up a fox by the huntsman's horn and voice, to celebrate the proper culmination of the hunt. The whoops and screeches that accompany a kill are usually recorded, on paper, as 'Who whoop!' The horn call is known as 'the rattle', and that describes it very well. The huntsman will be dancing about around the hounds, whooping and rattling, and encouraging them to 'worry, worry, worry', and to 'tear him, and eat him'. If he is not excited, and pleased for his

The Cattistock hounds after catching a fox in a reed bed in Dorset

hounds, he is a pretty miserable huntsman. There is a sad story
of a huntsman whose hounds had not caught a fox for a very
long time, but who happened to be on the spot when a hound
grabbed a fox by the end of its brush. The huntsman immediately leapt off his horse, and started tootling; the hound
was so astonished that it loosed the fox, who promptly disappeared. We all told the hapless man that he had invented a new
horn call, the 'got away'.

It may be that you will want to mark the successful end of
your hunt with a memento – a brush, or even a mask (head) to
hang in your hall; it could cause quite a talking point on the
occasion of the next visit by the Townswomen's Guild. If you
are too shy to ask, get someone to do it for you; the huntsman
will normally be happy to oblige, and it is customary to slip
him a quid, or at least buy him a drink. A brush is easily cured;

you just stick it in a milk bottle of methylated spirits for at least
three weeks. A mask is a different matter; it requires the skill of
a good taxidermist (a badly mounted mask looks dreadful) and
will set you back £50-70.

WINTER HUNTING IN GENERAL

Marking and stopping

If hounds run their fox to ground you will hear them 'marking', and the huntsman encouraging them to 'leu wind him, leu
wind him'. A good huntsman will allow his hounds to have a
good mark. There are those who say that a good mark is as
good as a kill to hounds; I do not accept that, but it is certainly
second best.

Marking to ground should not be a regular feature of hunting, in a well-run country. The aim should be for continuous
movement. The earths should be stopped. The fox is a noctur-
nal animal. In bad winter weather he tends to lie snug at home,
and venture out, at night, to dine. The aim of the management
should be to keep the foxes above ground, on hunting days;
and to this end, there will be a stopping system. There is usually a network of volunteers, each responsible for certain earths
when the hounds are in the area. The best time for stopping is
after the pubs shut, when the foxes are likely to be out. The
stopper simply goes to the earth, and blocks the holes.

'Simply' is not the best description; forcing your way
through a blackthorn thicket in pitch dark and driving rain,
locating all the holes by torchlight, then shovelling in grassy
earth with a slippery spade, is not simple. Human nature being
what it is, there is a tendency to hurry the job, and perhaps miss
a hole; or to take one look at the weather and decide that the job
would be better done in the morning, and daylight. 'Putting
to', as this is called, has the disadvantage of being more than
likely to stop the fox in, which means that he will stay snugly at
home until the next night, and miss the star appearance for
which he had been billed, the next day. Good stopping un-

Marking to ground

doubtedly makes for good hunting, but there are countries where the terrain is such as to preclude comprehensive stopping, and where good terrier work is a necessary part of the day's sport.

During regular hunting, when the aim is to keep the customers on the move, long digs should be out. If there is a good chance of the fox being bolted quickly, this may be worth

a try, especially if there is some doubt about finding another
fox quickly. Even so, no more than quarter of an hour should
be allowed, before the master decides to draw again. Winter
days are short, and people are entitled to have as much hunting
as is possible crammed into the day.

Inconclusive days

A lot of hunts finish inconclusively when the line of the fox
weakens unto vanishing point; however patient and persever-
ing huntsman and hounds may be, it is all a matter of scent.
You were misguided if you thought that every hunting day
would consist of non-stop galloping. There will be days when
you will hardly go out of a walk, and days when every fox the
hounds find seems to promptly disappear into the ether. There
will be occasions when there are no foxes to be found, so that
covert after covert is drawn blank, and iron enters into the collective soul. There is never any certainty of good sport. It is the
uncertainty of hunting that is part of its fascination, and, as a
sportsman, you must learn to accept that. Remember that all
hunting consists of hunting a wild animal, in natural conditions
which are infinitely variable. There is no doubt that some
huntsmen, and their hounds, make better use of the prevailing
conditions than others do, but all are subject to the vagaries of
scent and weather. If you take some interest in the hounds, as
well as the riding, even a moderate day can be interesting. The
best hound work happens on a bad scenting day, and if you are
able to watch and appreciate the performance, it will compen-
sate for the fact that you have never gone out of a trot, or left
the ground, all day.

If you hunt in a car, or on foot, the work of the hounds will
be your main interest, and you will be very keen to get yourself
in the best position to achieve this end. It has to be said that the
aims of the car followers and the mounted followers are by no
means always complementary. If you want to get a good view
of the fox and hounds, the best way is to work out where the
fox is going, and some people are brilliant at this, and get there

before him. Nine times out of ten this will mean that the fox gets headed, that is diverted from his chosen course. This is undesirable, firstly because, from a sporting point of view, the fox should be allowed to go where he wants to go. It is also undesirable because had the fox been able to cross the road that had been effectively blocked by fifty cars, he might have gone straight on down into the vale, and produced a super hunt. Because he has been headed, he may well take the huff, and head for the back gardens of a village, where the hunt will finish inconclusively and in a muddle.

It should be thought of as a crime to head a fox, whether you are mounted or on foot, and if you do, the master may well be inclined to address a few well-chosen words to you on the matter. But all rules are made to be broken, and there are times when a fox definitely should be headed; such as when he is heading for a motorway, or main railway, or anywhere where hounds might be in danger. I remember helplessly watching hounds running hard along the main Plymouth to London railway line, and turning off it seconds before the up Cornish Riviera express thundered into the cutting. We were lucky, but it would have been much better if the fox, and therefore the hounds, had been diverted from the line altogether.

In an emergency, everyone should use their best endeavours to stop hounds. This is easier said than done, and the better the hounds and the better the scent, the more difficult it is. Hounds are not easily diverted from their fox, and should never be stopped off with whip cracking and rough words, except in a real emergency. They do not understand about main roads; all they know is that there is a fox in front of them, and here is some idiot trying to prevent them getting to it. There are some hunts where whips are cracked a lot, and you may feel that you should be macho, and have a go too. In a well-run hunt you will hear no whip cracking, and I do not advise you to attempt to start it, or rather I do; the sight of you attempting to crack a whip when neither you, nor your horse, are used to it should provide great entertainment all round.

Length of day and second horses

The length of the hunting day can be pretty elastic, and will vary from country to country. An old management will tend to pack up earlier than one that is young and keen. The general rule is that hounds should not draw for a fox unless there will be enough daylight left to hunt and catch him by. In the north during December and early January, hounds will seldom draw after 3.30pm; whilst further south and west it may well be possible to stretch the day to 4.30, or even 5.00. It is not a good thing to lose your hounds in the dark. In most low-ground countries, it is nearly always possible to get to their heads, and pick them up. It is not so easy in the hills. I have many times watched my hounds disappearing into the dusk, being prevented by the nature of the ground from getting anywhere near them. Hounds running hard in the frosty moonlight is a marvellous sound, but it would be much preferred if they were tucked up snug, and warm, in the kennels.

It is certainly the duty of the masters to make the most of the day, and not give up too easily. Much will depend on the day. If the weather is foul, with no scent and the foxes very sensibly going absent, there is little sense in prolonging the misery, and trailing hounds and horses about to no good purpose. In these circumstances, a sensible master will turn to his shivering supporters, and suggest that, whilst he is duty bound to continue if they so wish, it is his opinion that little good will come of continuing, and would those who want to go home please show. Hunting is supposed to be fun, and there are some days when it jolly well is not.

Sometimes there will be a hunt of such splendour early in the day that anything after would be an anticlimax; it is a good thing to quit while you are ahead. I remember a day when by 1.30 we had killed three foxes, and the horses had been reduced to a walk; there was nothing to do but go home. I was a real killing scent that day, and how I longed for a second horse. It is your horse power that will decide the length of your day. If you bottom your horse in the morning, you will miss the after-

noon hunt. Remember that scenting conditions will usually improve in the late afternoon, when the air temperature cools whilst the ground temperature stays warm; this is when hounds will really run, and the best sport of the day often happens after 2.30, when all the weaker brethren have gone home to tea.

If you hunt in a galloping country, and can afford it, a second horse is a great thing. A tired horse is more inclined to damage itself, and its rider. If you really bottom a horse, it may be a long time before it pulls out again. The problem with a second horse is having someone to ride it for you, and to produce it where and when you want it, in full fig of condition. What you do not want is someone like the Irish second horseman who, when asked why the second horse was in a somewhat less than fresh condition, replied that it was no wonder for the horse had jumped fence for fence with His Honour's horse in the recent hunt. The smarter hunts overcome this problem by having the second horses at a prearranged spot, which they then repair to, even if it means stopping hounds. They will not admit it, but what they then do is stop for lunch, and having blocked all the road for half an hour, and browsed and sluiced, they mount their second horse for the afternoon session. You should not allow all the smart people to make you think that this is correct behaviour; it is very suburban. Good hunting, to repeat, should be perpetual motion, and the correct way of changing horses should reflect this urgency.

I have been blessed with some first-class second horsemen, who had the knack of dropping out of the sky, just when needed. The correct drill is this. The second horse should pull up on the off side of your horse, by which time its leathers should be at your length, and the girth tight. The man leaps off on the off side, and takes both horses by the head. Drop your reins, hands on the withers of the second horse, vault across (a little practice at home will not come amiss), feet in irons, gather up reins, cast off forrard – and away. Total time should be about 30 seconds.

Going to a holloa

Notes on the months

November is very often a bad hunting month, for scent depends on the weather and November weather is often unsettled and stormy, which conditions are bad for scent. There is also the problem of fallen leaves. Freshly fallen ones spoil the scent in covert, which makes it difficult to put pressure on the fox in the vital early stages of a hunt: 'a fox well found, is a fox half killed'. So November sport may be somewhat disappointing, which may be as well for those who have not bothered to get their horses fit. I well remember a November when all the hunt horses went down with the cough the day before the opening meet. We had to borrow horses. This was not a great problem for the slightly built whipper-in; for me riding 17 stone, it was another matter altogether. In fact, there was only one horse in the country available to me. It was a particularly bad scenting November, and it is the only time that I have been grateful for bad hunting.

Things tend to brass up in December. The weather settles down, and gets a bit cooler. You can normally look forward to some good hunting up to Christmas. What I regard as the two greatest hunts of my career, both happened in early December. In the first one we found a fox at 11.20, and killed him 4½ hours, and 25 miles, later. It was one of those lovely scenting days when hounds never actually go very fast, but they never stop; they just keep going and going, and you have time to watch them and appreciate all the subtleties of the hunt. The other thing I shall never forget about that day, was the cry at the end. When hounds are running a beaten fox, and they know that he is beaten (I suppose the scent tells them), the cry changes; we call it a 'killing cry', and it is quite unmistakable. This day, as hounds dropped down into the steep valley where they caught their fox, the cry changed: it was such cry as I have never heard before or since. Perhaps the acoustics in the valley helped; I tell you it made my back hairs stand up; it was such a savage, triumphant sound.

The other hunt took place on my birthday. There were a lot of people out, and we had a morning when everything went wrong. About half-past one, we drew a little patch of kale, and a great, big dog fox went away. This day we had a 10½-mile point (18 as hounds ran), crossed two main rivers, ran right through our neighbouring hunt's country, and in fact ran into the next hunt but one, who were collecting their hounds, in the dusk, which brought matters to a conclusion. It was just as well, because the four of us who got to the end were struggling to cross a steep wooded valley, and we would have lost our hounds in the dark, had they not been stopped. It was probably the best birthday present that I could have been given; although I wish my hounds could have had their fox.

Boxing Day is a great show day. Boxing Day meets tend to happen in strange places, like in front of the Guildhall in the town centre. Hundreds of cars, and thousands of people, turn out for the only day's hunting in their year; roads are blocked solid for miles, and the chances of decent sport are slim indeed.

Nevertheless, you should turn out, to fly the flag, and you never know. I can remember a few, only a few, cracking good hunts on Boxing Day: if you are not there, you will not get them when they do happen.

We must not pass Christmas without mentioning Christmas boxes. The Boxing Day cap is divided amongst the hunt staff, and people are expected to dig fairly deep into the wallet. If you hunt regularly, you may well wish to record your appreciation of these splendid people in a more personal way, by giving them your contribution, and thanking them yourself; it is the correct thing to do. How much should you give? You cannot give too much; but if you want a guide, I suggest that a tithe of your hunt subscription should be the very minimum. And do not forget the backroom boys, and girls, of the kennels and stables. They work long hours to produce your sport, and are a long way from being over paid; they will appreciate your appreciation of the work that they do.

January is a problem month, and the extent of the problem may well depend on which part of Britain you hunt in. You would think that you are more likely to encounter bad weather in the north than the south. I was bred in Cornwall, and do not remember seeing snow until I was seven years old; and that was gone by lunch time. In the past few years, there seems to have been worse weather in the south and west of England, than in the north. But I suppose the nearer you hunt to the Gulf Stream, the warmer (and wetter) you are likely to be.

Snow is a problem. If the snow is dry, and powdery, it is perfectly possible to ride in it; the trouble is that you cannot see what you are riding over, and it certainly adds a piquancy to the jumping of fences. Wet snow balls up in the hoof, and this can be dangerous. Hounds, however, are not affected by snow, and most hunts will continue hunting on foot if the conditions are not suitable for horses. It is usually sensible to confine hunting in these conditions to the woods, as it is often impossible to get about in the open, especially if the snow has drifted up the gates. You should also remember that snow

causes considerable stress amongst livestock and their owners; additional disturbance by hounds may not be welcome. It is fair to say that hunting continues in the north in conditions that would not be regarded as possible in the south.

Frost is more of a problem. Ice can damage horses, hounds, and people, and is thoroughly undesirable. You should be prepared for a lay off, sometime in the new year. I must admit that I think that a week's rest, in a long season, does no harm at all; remember that in some countries hounds have already been hunting for five months.

In a bad time, the whole of January may be a write off. This is a pity because January, and February, can be the best hunting months, weather permitting. Many litters of cubs are born in March and April, which means that they are conceived in January and February. Dog foxes will come to a mating vixen from miles around; these 'travelling dogs' produce the best hunts. For a starter, they smell strong; secondly, when found by hounds the instinct of a visiting dog is to head for home, which may be many miles away. This is when you get your good 'points', and finish up in unexpected places. I remember asking a farmer friend whether he was coming hunting the next day. He replied that he was not going to waste a day in the big woods, where we were bound, at the far corner of the country; he was going out with the neighbours, who were in a good place. He went out with the neighbours, and they never found a fox. He returned home in tatty fettle, which was not improved by finding me and my hounds sitting in his yard, having run 20 miles, with a 9-mile point. His face when he saw us, is a memory which I will always treasure. It is worth remembering that the best hunts often happen from the most unlikely places – another example of the glorious uncertainty of hunting.

9
Hunting in Spring

As a general rule, you will have had the best of the hunting by the end of February. Indeed, there are many countries where the pressures of modern farming bring hunting to a close early in March. Most foxhounds finish their season during that month. A minority are able to continue into, and through, April, and only a handful still seek to kill a May fox.

March is something of a problem. As the month goes on, the huntable country becomes more and more restricted. It is really only those countries with big woods, or hills, who can hope to carry on until April. March is an all or nothing month: you can have some really good days: and some really bad ones. The whole thing becomes a bit 'fag endy'. Scent is rarely good. The ground is beginning to dry out, there is fresh tillage, the weather begins to get warmer (and then drops a blizzard on you), and the equinoctial gales are hardly conducive to good sport.

The foxes tend to disappear. This is perfectly natural, and a protective measure. The vixens are heavy, or may even have cubs; whatever, they tend to lie to ground, and the dog foxes

will often lie up with them. This means that hounds can draw miles of country, which a short time before was lifting with foxes, and find nothing. Worse still, hounds may mark at earth after earth, and have to be taken away time after time, which is damaging for their morale. From the sporting point of view, there should be no terrier work after the middle of March: pregnant and nursing mothers should be left in peace. From a practical point of view this is not always possible; especially in the hills. Foxes do kill young lambs, which do represent a handy food source for a growing family. Hill shepherds look to their local hunt to see that the lambing damage is kept to a minimum. It is sometimes necessary to destroy vixen, and a litter. This is not sport, and there is no pleasure in it. But it is better if a clean job is done by experts, than if the job is bungled by amateurs.

As March progresses, there is the increasing worry about lambing ewes. For the farmer, lambing is a time of maximum worry, and minimal sleep, with consequent nervous fragmentation. However keen on hunting a man may be, he certainly does not want hounds through his lambing field.

By the end of March, hounds, horses, men and country have all grown stale, and most hunts are right to finish then. However, you say to yourself, I am well, my horse is well, and I want more hunting; what now shall I do? Your choice is limited. You will have to go north, or west.

STAGHUNTING ON EXMOOR

You can go buckhunting (fallow) in the New Forest, or you can go staghunting (red deer) on the Quantocks or Exmoor. This continues right through April, and as the young stags are hunted at this time of year, there can be some spectacular hunts. Deer hunting is completely different to fox, or harehunting, and has a chapter of its own. It is certainly a spring hunting option that you should consider. I deeply regret that time, and distance, no longer allow me to visit Exmoor in

spring. If you make the journey, you will meet hunting people from all over the world, and enjoy the Exmoor hospitality, if you have the stamina. As mentioned in Chapter 3, some people do not like the idea of staghunting, but I have never heard anyone who has actually done it say that. You have to see it for yourself to appreciate how much the people of Exmoor understand and love the deer which are so much a part of their daily life. If you go to Exmoor and district, you will be able to hunt fox as well. Indeed, if stamina, purse, and horse flesh allow, you would still be able to hunt 5 days in the 7, and possibly 6.

You may wish to take your own horse(s), quite a lot of people do, so a word of caution is in order. Do not expect to turn up on spec, and find accommodation for horse and rider. A sizeable chunk of hunting Britain packs its bags and heads for the west in spring, and stabling and beds should be arranged well in advance. I know that you have hunted your horse all season and that it is fit, but unless it is used to hills I am afraid that it will blow up in short order; always reckon that it takes a horse a full hunting season to learn to cope with hill hunting, and you must make the appropriate allowances. If going up hill is a problem, going downhill is another. Do not be deceived by the way the hardy hill men gallop downhill with careless abandon, they, and their horses, are used to it; you should proceed with rather more caution. If you attempt to gallop up the hills you will soon bottom your horse. The rule is to allow it to go up hill at its own pace; you can go down the other side as fast as you like.

It is possible to hire horses on Exmoor, but they do not come cheap and demand tends to exceed supply, so you would be well advised to book well ahead. With local hirelings you will at least be certain of safe and locally experienced horses, which may allow you to enjoy the scene all the more.

FELL HUNTING

Perhaps you do not want to be bothered with horses, and want something completely different, in which case you will have to

The Eskdale & Ennerdale Hunt in rugged country in the Lake District

lift up your eyes unto the high hills. In the north of England and Wales (and in certain parts of Scotland) there are packs of foxhounds who go quietly about their business of foxcatching with little of the pageantry, or flummery, which can be attached to mainstream hunting. For the sake of convenience we will refer to these as the 'fell packs'. These hounds are hunted, and followed, on foot; the sort of terrain that they hunt making any other form of transport impracticable, unless you wish to drive round the valley roads. Sheep are the main agricultural output of these countries, and provide the main source of livelihood for most of the local inhabitants, including the foxes; whereby a clash of interests may arise.

The fell packs have been hunted and bred on their own traditional lines since, and long before, the time of the famous John Peel. John Peel has become famous through the song about him, which almost everybody knows a bit of. But the song, and the man, are only a small part of a famous oral tradition that is part of the local culture of the Lake District. Every famous fell huntsman, every great hunt, every famous hound and terrier, features in a song. These are not folk songs sung, in soulless nasal, by greasy girls with hairy legs; these are everyday work songs, part of an ongoing rural tradition. Some are very ancient, but new songs are composed every year about current heroes and happenings, and they are sung in the pubs, after hunting, when the 'tatty pot' supper is sitting nicely on the tum, and the ale is being supped. In these wild areas, hunting is not only a practical necessity, it is also the social catalyst that brings together people who live solitary lives on remote hill steadings.

In spring, hunting enthusiasts from all over the country head for the fells, and you could do a lot worse than follow them. You will see masters, and huntsmen, from many lowland packs; for the excellent qualities of the fell hound, who has never been subject to whims of fashion, are becoming increasingly appreciated. Fell and Welsh lines are finding their way into many discerning low-ground kennels.

Fell hunting is a bit of a lottery. Some days you can stand in one place, and see an entire day's hunting. On other days, hounds will find a fox 'gan oot over', and you will never see them again that day. Most days will be somewhere in between. There may be long periods without sight or sound of a hound, and then, on a distant ridge, you will see a string of tiny white dots 'coming in', and you can heave a sigh of relief if you have sufficient breath. Breath is very important. There are two ways you can tackle fell hunting: foot, or car. Remember that, unless you are basically fit, you should not be too ambitious about the walking. The locals who make a 1,000-foot climb look fairly effortless are doing it all the time, and they can go down the rocks on the other side like mountain goats. If you are as fit as the next man, which is probably not very, take your time; climb a bit of high ground, and watch, and listen. At least you will have a lovely view, and the virtuous feeling of having taken violent exercise. Two words of caution; firstly do not set out on the fells poorly clad – T-shirt and trainers will not do. The temperature drops by one degree for every 300 feet that you climb. Spring weather in the hills is notoriously fickle; you can be in bright sunshine one moment, and in a raging blizzard five minutes later, so be sensible. Secondly, if you do get lost, remember that every stream runs down to the lowland; follow it and you may not get off the hill where you want to be, but you will get off somewhere.

Many of the locals now follow by car, especially the halt and the lame. The roads run in the valley bottoms. If hounds go out, you have the choice of either driving round to the next valley, which may mean a trip of twelve miles on twisty roads, or of staying put; it is a gamble. It is frustrating to drive many miles to be told that hounds have just gone out again, very likely back to where you have just come from. The choice will probably depend on your temperament.

CB Radio has taken some of the guesswork out of this. Most country people now have CB; it is extremely useful in remote areas. There was initial doubt, amongst traditionalists, about

Fell hunting

the application of this particular product of science to hunting. My opinion is that if I can get in on a hunt through the use of CB, which I would have missed without it, then I am for it.

The fell packs usually finish their regular hunting early in April. They then go 'on call' for the hill lambing which usually starts about 20 April. Hill lambs are at their most vulnerable to foxes during the first week of life when they are comparatively feeble; they are especially vulnerable at birth, in the dark, and in confusion. A determined hill ewe is more than a match for a fox, but suppose she has twins; who will guard little wobbly No 1, whilst she is straining with No 2? This is when the damage is often done. Not every fox will take lambs, but once a fox starts, it will return again and again to this useful food source.

Foxes seldom mess on their own doorstep. Many old shepherds say that the safest place to have a litter of cubs is hard by the lambing field. The resident vixen will not only respect her host, but will also discourage others from miring her pitch. However, lambs get taken, and the hunt is sent for.

When hounds are on call, there are no regular fixtures: it is strictly a fire-alarm business, and the calls are dealt with on a first come, first served, basis. The huntsman will only take a few trusted old hounds. At first light he will go to the troubled lambing field, and draw round the periphery. The aim is to pick up the overnight drag of the lamb killer, and hunt away to where she is lying. It is not impossible to meet the fox in person, if she is late leaving the scene of the crime. The fox is hunted until she is either killed, or holed. If she goes to ground then every effort is made to kill her; sport is not the main consideration on this occasion. Once the fox is accounted for, whether after 30 minutes, or 6 hours, the day is finished. In a busy time, hounds can be out 6 days out of 6.

Hounds continue on call for as long as is necessary; often well into May. By the nature of this sort of work, it may not be known one day where hounds will be the next. Most places where you stay in the Lakes will be geared up to finding out where the hounds are going to be, and visitors are usually welcome. Just remember that the object of the exercise has nothing to do with entertaining you, and you will just have to make the best of whatever the day brings. A fine spring morning on the high fells, is a reward in itself; and if it is blowing a gale, with horizontal sleet, at least you can turn round and go back to bed; the huntsman cannot. Think on that; and buy him a dram when you see him in the pub.

MINK AND OTTER HUNTING

The two sports that we have not considered are mink hunting, and otter hunting. These are really summer sports, but they tend to get started in spring.

Otter hunting no longer happens in Great Britain. The otter
is a shy, elusive creature, and during the seventies its population went into a rapid decline for various reasons. There was an
increase in water pollution both industrial and agricultural,
which was very damaging to all water-based wildlife. At the
same time the various water and drainage authorities got
thoroughly over-excited about tidying up and 'rationalising'
their various streams and rivers; much rough land was drained
and brought into production to help build the grain alps. The
poor old otter had his home drained, and drag-lined, out of
existence. Merry animal lovers started 'liberating' farm mink.
These vicious little creatures thrived, and multiplied, and
further upset the delicate ecological balance of which the otter
was a part.

The upshot of all this 'progress' was that the otter rapidly declined, and disappeared, over the bulk of the British Isles.
Faced with this crisis the Masters of Otterhounds Association
met and decided that all otter hunting should cease; it did, and
the otter is now a protected animal. The otter's habitat has not
returned, and otters are now largely confined to the remoter
parts of Britain, which nobody can be bothered to improve
much.

If you want to go otter hunting, and it is perhaps the most
scientific and difficult (and therefore most interesting) form of
hunting, you will have to go to County Cork in Eire, where the
two remaining otter hunts operate – the Bride View, and the
Cork City. It has already been mentioned that Cork City
apparently boasts no less than five trencher-fed packs of
hounds, with the hounds being kept on the housing estates in
and around the city: what a truly proud municipal record.

In Great Britain, the otterhound packs took to doing a useful job dealing with the liberated mink, who were multiplying
into a real menace. Mink are vicious and wanton killers, and
appear to be omnivorous. I have never been mink hunting, because no pack operates in the area where I live: I wish they did.
It is not sport of the calibre of otter hunting; in fact it might

possibly be compared to ratting on a larger scale; even so I would point out that the late, great Duke of Beaufort always considered that ratting was second only to foxhunting in the scale of excellences.

Mink and otter are semi-aquatic animals: it therefore follows that the hunting of them takes place in, and around, water, and on foot. At the very least, following the mink hounds will give you the chance to walk some lovely rivers, and to see parts of the countryside that most people never see. Even if hounds never find, you will see much pleasant scenery and lots of wildlife – some of it very wild indeed, like the naked couple who burst out of one end of a riparian thicket after the Hawkstone Otterhounds had gone in the other; they were truly wild.

The basic principles of both sports are the same: hounds draw along the banks of a river, or stream, until they either hit off an overnight drag, or mark in a bankside hole. The scent of the otter is the strongest of any hunted creature, and the drag can be up to twenty-four hours old. A whole day can be spent hunting a drag without ever actually coming up to the otter. This does not really matter; there is still the hound work to watch, and listen to, and gentle ambulatory exercise going on. You stop for lunch too, so take some sandwiches, or arrange for your man to follow in the limo, with the hamper.

It is perfectly possible to cover ten or fifteen miles during a day's otter hunting, which can lead to the fragmentation of family groups. I remember a day in Devon, when we had covered many miles, and at the end of the day a child was absent. As luck would have it, there was present the local doyen of otter hunters, a man of unparalleled local knowledge and wisdom. He would surely know the best place to seek the lost boy. The situation was put to him as he sat in his car pulling on dry socks and shoes (note this: always take a change of kit with you). A thoughtful expression formed on the craggy slopes of this face. He lit his pipe. We all waited, hardly daring to breathe. You could see the pronouncement coming, rather

in the way that you can see a sheep bringing up its cud to chew.

'Lost a boy?'

'Yes! Yes!' we all cried, chewing our knuckles.

'Terrible thing to lose a boy in Devon', he said; and getting into his little car, phuttered off into the sunset. (The boy incidentally, was alive and well.)

The thing with the otter's drag is that you are never quite sure which end of it you are on. It is quite possible that hounds are hunting away from the quarry. As a I understand it, this is not quite such a problem with mink. They are smaller and have nothing like the range of the otter; by the same token, when they are found, they are unlikely to supply the same standard of hunting. It seems that the ambition of the mink is to find a hole as quickly as possible, from which it will have to be evicted with terriers and spades. This makes for rather stop/go hunting. But what does it matter on a fine spring or summer day. You are out with hounds, in good company, and in pleasant places; if you were not there, you would only be working, or polishing the car.

10
Scent

If you have never read *Handley Cross*, by R. S. Surtees, you should lose no time in obtaining a copy. Mr Jorrocks, the Cockney grocer and Master of Foxhounds, is one of the great comic characters of literature. His dicta are often quoted by hunting people, and one of his most famous is undoubtedly that 'there's nothing so queer as scent, 'cept a woman'. Peace be unto all you feminists; it is your unpredictability that Jorrocks is referring to. All hunting is done by scent, and yet no one really understands it, and I rather hope they never do: it is because it is so unpredictable that hunting is so interesting.

So, what is scent, I have heard it described as microscopic droplets that are left by the quarry. The strength of those droplets, and how they are affected by the current ground and air conditions, will determine the strength of the scent. The inbred sensitivity and physical condition of the hound's nose, will determine how well the scent is interpreted. Thus many, many factors combine to determine whether you have a good scenting day, or not.

Where does scent come from? Very roughly, it may be

divided into three categories: pad scent, body scent, and breath scent. The fox has scent glands at the root of the brush (as does your dog; hence all that sniffing), and sweat glands in his pads. He does not sweat through the skin, but through mouth and pads. There are glands in the body but they are to do with a secretion for keeping the coat glossy; although they are all part of the scent total. The nervous system controls the sweat glands, and the excretion of the tiny droplets that were mentioned earlier. The faster a fox goes the more he is likely to smell, and the harder the hounds are able to hunt him. Foxes live by scent, and they know exactly what the conditions are on any day. This is why, on a good scenting day, a fox will go away like a bullet, and keep travelling; while on a bad scenting day, he knows there is little urgency and will dawdle along, adjusting his pace to the prevailing conditions. It is obvious that a fox is more likely to be killed on a good scenting day. The better the scent, the faster he will have to move, and the more he will sweat, thereby increasing the output of scent from all sources. On a good scenting day, the pressure of the on coming hounds will force the fox to maintain a fairly straight course which, in turn, makes it easier for hounds to hunt him. On a bad scenting day, the fox will have time to twist and turn, and hounds are likely to lose a little time at each turn. Lots of little losses add up to a big loss of time, during which the scent is continually deteriorating. Hounds can never go faster than their noses allow them to.

The scent of the fox is affected by many factors. It is quite common for hounds to draw over a fox without finding him. A fox gives off very little scent when he is lying still, probably just a little breath scent. It is a fact that if a fox is chased by a cur dog (such as a collie) during a hunt, he never carries the same scent thereafter. No one has ever really been able to account for this phenomenon. One theory is that the scent of the dog cancels out the scent of the fox but, as the chase is usually a short one, that does not account for the fact that the scent of the fox continues to be poor after the dog has faded. It may be some

The fox

glandular defence mechanism, triggered by the sudden onslaught of the dog, but then why is the mechanism not triggered by hounds in the first place?

There are other natural defence mechanisms. A heavy vixen usually has very little scent, which is good; yet by some perverse twist, a milking vixen often has a strong scent. I cannot help but feel that nature slipped up there somewhere.

The more tired a hunted fox becomes, the less he smells. This again is a natural defence. If you know the hounds, you will see that, towards the end of a hunt, the old ones who have perhaps been slightly outpaced by their younger colleagues in the faster early stages, come to the fore. The main reason for this is probably that their more experienced noses are required to unravel the increasingly difficult scent, and that experience also tells them that the fox is sinking. A great number of foxes are lost in the final stages of a hunt. The strong smell of a fresh fox may well seduce all, or most, of the pack. The old saying is that if

hounds divide, the smaller lot is nearly always right. This is because the smaller set is nearly always composed of the old and
bold, who refused to relinquish the failing scent of the run fox
for the smellier blandishments of the new. Certain foxhound
bloodlines are noted for transmitting the virtue of 'non
change'. These lines are fine gold to huntsmen who want to
catch the hunted fox. The best 'non change' line that I have experienced, is the New Forest Medyg '69, which is also my
favourite all-round fox-catching line.

Tired foxes can often seem to vanish into thin air, and the
closing stages of a hunt often require extreme care, and
patience, on the part of a huntsman. You should never lift
hounds off the line of a beaten fox. This is because to break
their concentration in the crucial final stages can be fatal – but
not for the fox. On one occasion, a tired fox was viewed only a
short distance in front of hounds, who were hunting steadily.
The huntsman got over-excited and, picking up the hounds,
galloped them to where he had seen the fox. Zero; he had
broken the concentration, got them off their noses and invited
them to look instead, and there was nothing to be seen. He
then had to persuade his excited hounds to tune their noses in
again, and precious minutes slipped away whilst they settled
down; all the while the scent was deteriorating, and the fox was
slipping further away. That fox was never caught, but I will lay
you a guinea to a gooseberry, that had that man contained his
excitement and left his hounds alone, they would have killed
that fox within the next ten minutes.

Another time, hounds had hunted steadily, and persever-
ingly, over some twelve miles of open hill. For much of that
time the fox had been plainly visible to the followers, who were
able to watch every twist and turn of the hounds. At last they
checked on a piece of open hill, where the fox had last been
seen. They cast, and cast again, making good all the ground,
without a whimper. Yet is seemed that, had the fox gone on, he
must have been seen. There were no holes for him to creep
into; it appeared that he had just vanished. The huntsman had

little wit, but he had enough to do absolutely nothing; which may have been because he had not a clue as to what to do anyway. There was a clump of rough grass which hounds had passed, and repassed, in their casting. One old dog had come back to this clump, and was watching it with his head on one side, and his stern just waving uncertainly.

'What is it Rector?', said the huntsman; 'Woof' said Rector, and the fox came vertically out of the tussock like an intercontinental ballistic missile. That fox did not get away. I hope that these two anecdotes illustrate the difficulties of scent.

A fox's scent is affected by diet, so that the same fox will have a different scent according to what he has been eating. Many people consider that rabbit-fed foxes carry the strongest scent, but I have no idea how they know. Dustbin foxes, that live in and around housing areas and live mainly on domestic detritus, carry very little scent. Both dog fox, and vixen, smell strongly after coitus.

However strongly a fox may smell, the distribution of that scent varies greatly. It is obvious that if a fox runs through a flock of sheep, or over ground that is freshly spread with pigs' slurry, its scent is going to be masked. A hound's nose is probably a thousand times more sensitive than yours, so if you can smell manure, imagine the effect it must have on hound senses; petrol and diesel fumes must be a positive irritant to their sensitive organs. Different types of soil have an effect. Fresh ploughing, and recently worked land, is bad for scent. Old pasture should be best, but if it is sour with stock it will not be as good as clean winter corn. Limestone land, and chalk, are bad scenting unless really wet. Most countries are better for a bit of moisture.

Wind obviously has an effect. Jorrocks advises against taking out hounds on a 'werry wet day', and he is right. If you think of scent as a thin vapour, it is not going to survive long in a force 8 gale. In most countries, the west, or south-west, winds are considered favourable to hunting, whilst the east wind, especially when accompanied by a 'blue haze', is con-

sidered bad. The great Lord Leconfield had a wind vane that registered on the ceiling of the library in Petworth House. If it stood east on a hunting day, the huntsman would be sent out with the hounds whilst His Lordship stayed snug by the fire. There are certain countries in north Yorkshire that are an exception; in those parts, you never get a good scent except on an easterly wind. There, when the wind is in the east; the sky can be bright and clear, except for a ragged rim of cloud around the horizon – a phenomenon called the 'Bridlington dogs'. When you see them on a hunting day, keep your hat rammed down and your girth tight.

In the 1930s, H. M. Budgett made an exhaustive study of scent, and wrote a book about it entitled. *Hunting by Scent*, of which I have never yet succeeded in getting a copy. He seems to have invented an instrument called a 'scentometer'. As I understand it, this machine had various dials marked with things like wind direction, barometric pressure, temperature, and I know not what else. You set the dials according to the prevailing conditions, and it gave a reading of the scent likely to maintain in those circumstances. However, as I suppose it to have been too cumbersome to carry about, it would not take account of conditions changing through the day. What Budgett did establish was that scent was governed by two main factors: the barometric pressure, and the temperature of the ground relative to their air. The earth breathes: sometimes drawing air into itself, sometimes exhaling, as it were. When the earth exhales, it is warmer than the air, and this is when hounds really run. Watch, when you are out hunting, how the mist starts to form in the watermeadows as the afternoon draws on; the air is cooling, and the ground is exhaling: check your girth. By the same token, hounds nearly always go like stink when there is a frost coming in. The reverse is true when a frost is coming out of the ground; the air is warmer than the ground, and scenting conditions will be tricky at best.

A falling barometer is bad for scent. The atmosphere is likely to be stormy, and the air currents volatile. I have heard people

say that the hounds are useless, for they can smell the fox themselves. Think for a moment: if you are perched on a horse with
your nose some eight feet above the ground, and you can smell
the fox, it stands to reason that scent is not also going to be
available to hounds at ground level.

A steady, or rising, glass is better for scent. A nice settled
spell of weather usually brings good hunting, especially if it is
the right sort of weather for the time of year; spring-like
weather in January is not good for hunting. However, scent
confounds all predictions. I have vivid memories of a season
when there was virtually no rain from October to April; it was
the driest winter in living memory. It was also one of the best
scenting seasons that I have known. I remember a January day
of blazing sun, and heat, with the dust flying behind hounds on
the arable, and they were in overdrive all day. It seems
probable that it was the settled weather that produced the
scent, in spite of the dryness and unseasonable warmth.

There are a number of signs that you can look out for that
may give you some indication of the likely scenting conditions;
I will put it no more strongly than that:

If everything looks clear and still, and the hedges stand out
thick and black, you are justified in being hopeful.
Gossamer webs are a bad sign.
Hounds rolling at the meet is a bad sign.
A westerly wind, and enough blue sky 'to mend a Dutch-
man's breeches' can indicate a useful sort of hunting day.
Stormy days are bad; especially when the weather breaks
after a settled spell.
Hounds eating grass, and vomiting, on the way to the meet
is a good sign.
Soft snow is often good for scenting.

Many people have their own (and sometimes unusual) ways
of estimating scent. A friend of mine reckoned that if he could
smell the local slaughterhouse when he first went out in the

morning, this was an infallible sign of a good scenting day. Another man considered the state of his armpits, when he got up, to be a good indication. I think that the only certain thing about scent is its uncertainty, and that, again, is part of the charm of hunting.

11
Deer Hunting

Deer hunting is so totally different to fox-, or hare-hunting that it deserves a chapter to itself. I have greatly enjoyed my days with the staghounds over the years, but I cannot claim any expertise in the subject and am greatly indebted to E. R. Lloyd for much of my information. Dick Lloyd is an acknowledged expert on the red deer of Exmoor, and on the hunting of them; you could be in no better hands.

There are at present four packs of hounds hunting wild deer in Great Britain: the New Forest Buckhounds who hunt the fallow deer of the New Forest and the Devon and Somerset, Quantock, and Tiverton Staghounds who hunt the red deer in north Devon and Somerset. In Ireland there are two packs of hounds who hunt carted stag: the Ward Union in Eire, and the County Down in Ulster.

CARTED STAG

Let us deal first with carted stag. This form of hunting no longer takes place in mainland Britain. It was very popular at

one time especially on the fringe of London, where it provided instant sport for tired business men. I remember meeting a very old man who could recall hunting with the Surrey Staghounds over Putney Vale. It seems that the last pack hunting carted stag in mainland Britain was the Norwich, who ceased to operate in the late sixties or early seventies.

It is an entirely artificial sport, in as much as the deer who are hunted are domesticated. The hunt's stock of deer are maintained in a special deer park. A deer is selected for the day, and driven to the meet in a van. He is then 'enlarged', or turned loose. Sometimes the deer throws a moody, and goes straight back into the box, in which case the day is a write off unless a spare deer is available. When the deer has been given sufficient law, the hounds are laid on, and a usually fast and furious hunt follows. When the deer gets bored he stops, the hounds bay him, the van comes up, the deer man puts a halter on the deer, and everyone goes home to tea including the deer, who returns to the park until his next turn for an outing. As a form of hunting it is, perhaps, a degree above draghunting, but the point is arguable.

ROE AND FALLOW DEER

There is a large wild deer population in mainland Britain. The roe deer is probably now the most numerous, its numbers having increased dramatically over the last twenty years. There are also increasing populations of sika and muntjac in parts of the country; these two species being originally park deer who have escaped and established themselves in their adopted country. The commonest park deer used to be the fallow. A deer park was as much a status symbol for a great house as an indoor heated pool is today. Many of the old deer parks have fallen into desuetude, and escapees from them have formed little wild colonies in various parts of the country.

The main concentration of wild fallow deer is in the New Forest, so called when William the Conqueror cleared out all

the hapless Saxon peasants who were scraping a living there and made it into a new royal hunting ground. It continued as a royal forest, and is currently administered by the Forestry Commission as agents of the Crown. The New Forest Buckhounds were founded in 1854, and hunt the fallow deer under licence from the deputy surveyor. They are the only hounds hunting fallow deer.

Roe deer hunting is an honourable tradition in France, but there are no hounds hunting roe in Britain at the present time, nor can I find any records of such a pack in recent history. This may be because roe deer were comparatively scarce until recent years.

RED DEER

The main part of the British red deer population is in the Highlands of Scotlands. There are isolated pockets in parts of England, but the highest concentration is in north Devon and west Somerset, and it is here that the three staghound packs operate. Exmoor has been a royal hunting forest from Norman times. The Ranger of Exmoor was a Crown office that probably maintained until 1818, when most of the Crown land on Exmoor was sold. The fortunes of the red deer have waxed and waned, according to the fortunes of hunting. There was a period in the middle of the last century when there was little, or no, organised sport and the red deer of Exmoor very nearly became extinct; today the population is put at 700 to 1,000. The red deer is our largest mammal. They are magnificent creatures, and you would have to be a very dull soul indeed not to be stirred by the sight of one.

Calves are usually born in midsummer; usually a single calf per hind. The calves are normally weaned by November. During his second year, the male deer will start growing his horns; the beam, or main stem, grows out of the skull in front of the ears. In the stag's third year he will grow points at the bottom of the beam; these are the 'brow' points. The next point up the

beam is called the 'bay', and the third one the 'trey'. At 5 years old he should have all these points on his antlers (and probably 2 on top); he is then said to have his 'rights'. By 8 years of age the stag is likely to have 3 on top, giving him a total of 12 points, which makes him a 'royal'; although it seems that this term is only used in Scotland. For the first 10 years of his life, the stag's antlers will grow in length, and strength, and produce more points on top. I understand that the Exmoor record is a 20 pointer. Each pair of antlers is unique. The number of points is a guide to age, but there can be variations, and it takes the experienced deer men to be accurate.

The stag sheds his antlers every year; usually in April or May. The horn starts to grow again at once, and grows throughout the summer. The new growth is extremely sensitive and liable to damage, being just a mass of blood vessels covered with a light skin known as 'velvet'. In August, the horn dries up and becomes solid. This process is apparently very irritating, and the stag takes to rubbing his horns on any solid object to remove the velvet, and allay the irritation. The solid object is often a tree, and considerable damage can be caused, especially in young plantations.

In October and November comes the rut, or mating time. The stags have spent the summer in bachelor groups, and male harmony. Now sex starts to rear its ugly head, the groups fragment, and each stag starts to look for mates. There is usually a dominant stag in each area, and his ambition is to gather unto himself as many hinds as possible, and thereafter to keep them. He proclaims his mastership by roaring defiance (belling), and backs up his Priapic claim with violence if necessary. Epic battles take place and deaths have been known to occur, although this is not thought to be a common occurrence. All this, not to mention the other, is pretty wearing; so towards the end of the period there will be increasing opportunity for the younger stags to nip in and carve themselves off a round or two.

Why hunt the deer? After all it does not raid hen houses, nor is there any recorded instance of deer taking young lambs. But

deer do cause considerable damage. North Devon and west Somerset are not like the Scottish Highlands. Stretches of moorland are interspersed with farms and wooded valleys. Through all this the wild deer roam, and feed, freely. At one time the only crop to be grown in this wet area was oats, but as we all know there has been an expansion of the growth of cereal crops into unlikely areas in recent years. Whatever the crop is, the deer are likely to eat it. The amount that they eat is quite insignificant to the amount that they spoil. Deer find cornfields very congenial places to lie up during the day, and what better than a good roll before you couch down after breakfast. Picture for yourself the state of a field of corn after twenty deer have used it as restaurant, gymnasium and rest room.

Swedes and turnips are an important winter feed for the stock farmer; the deer are also very partial to a nibble, and thereby hangs the problem. No one would mind much if the deer took the odd turnip, ate it, and went on his/her way, but this is not their wont. They nibble at the top of a turnip, until it becomes loose in the soil, then they discard it and start on a fresh one. The discarded and bitten turnips rot, and are then inedible to the sheep for whom they were intended in the first place. A herd of deer can lay waste a considerable flap of roots in one night, but the cost of erecting deer-proof fencing is immense and far beyond the resources of small stock-farmers.

Why then do they tolerate the deer? The answer, by and large, is because of the hunting. The red deer and the hunting of them is part of the local way of life. As football is to many urban dwellers, so staghunting is to Exmoor. When the staghounds meet, everything stops in the area. The happenings of the day are discussed with the same intensity as the day's play at Anfield or Cardiff Arms Park. The people are proud of their deer, and proud of their hounds, and rightly consider the one exists for, and because of, the other. The Devon and Somerset Staghounds also hold themselves responsible for deer damage, and help with temporary fencing, and scarers, to try to minimise damage. In cases of serious distress, some form of

compensation may be agreed upon. It also has to be said that the hunting attracts great numbers of visitors to the region all of whom have to be housed and fed, and often their horses as well; all of which provides a useful source of income.

The hunting of the red deer can be divided into three stages: autumn staghunting, hindhunting, spring staghunting. The autumn staghunting takes place in August, September and October. In this phase only the old stags, of five years or more, are hunted. Easy to say, but how do you go about selecting your stag, and then get him to cooperate? This is where the harbourer comes in.

The harbourers are men of respect. They are usually farmers, and all have tremendous knowledge and experience of the wild deer. When the hounds are to meet at point X, the harbourer sets out the day before, making use of his local knowledge and local information, to find a warrantable (huntable) stag. We have already discussed the ways of telling a stag's age, but bear in mind that these men really know their local deer, as a shepherd knows his flock. They will probably have known a particular stag from his youth upwards. The deer will have been lying up during the day, and the harbourer will set out on a tour of vantage places where he knows he has a good chance of observing a stag when he comes out to feed in the evening. When he has spied a suitable stag he will watch him until dark. In the old days he would probably have curled up under a tree root, eaten the bit of bait in his pocket and slept alfresco. In these enlightened times, with modern transport, he can pop home or bed down at a handy steading.

Whatever, he will be back on station before dawn, and hope to see his stag again at first light, when the animal will finish feeding. The harbourer wants to see where his quarry is going to lie up for the day. If the stag has already retired, the harbourer will have to slot (track) the stag by his slots, or footprints. To an expert a slot is almost as individual as a set of antlers. If the stag is lying up in a bracken bed, or some sheltered open bank, the harbourer may well be able to spy

him; although, even with powerful glasses, this is not always easy to the unpractised eye. If the stag has bedded in a covert, the man will not be able to see him, and will have to verify his presence by slotting again; what goes in can also come out, as many an inexperienced person has discovered to his personal chagrin. Once certain as to where the stag is lying, and that he is settled, the harbourer sets off for the meet.

At the meet, the harbourer reports to the masters and the huntsman. It is more than likely that the chosen stag will be lying with other deer; he has to be separated from them, and persuaded to leave his bedchamber. This may be no simple operation, and is a job for the old and bold. The pack is kennelled either in a horse box, or a convenient barn. Three or four couple of the oldest and wisest hounds are drawn out; these are the tufters.

The tufters are taken to rouse the chosen stag and get him away from the other stags and off, travelling by himself. This may take ten minutes, or some hours. You will not generally be encouraged to go with the tufters; unskilled personnel may well get in the way. From a practical point of view, you may well knacker your horse before the hunt proper actually starts. Remember the huntsman will have two, or even three, horses available for the day; you have not. You will find that most people take up a vantage point handy to where the main pack are kennelled. It is always a good principle to get off your horse whenever possible out hunting, on the same principle as you take your rucksack off when you have a breather; do this while you are waiting, and watch and listen.

When the tufters have got the stag away, they are stopped, and the pack is sent for. You will suddenly be aware of a man galloping hard towards you, blowing a whistle. The whipper-in, who has been leaning against the barn door smoking a fag, suddenly becomes action man. Away goes the fag; he is into the saddle, and galloping off with the pack, whilst you are still hopping about with one foot in the stirrup iron. The pack are taken to the huntsman, and laid on the line; the hunt is on.

Old stags get cunning and, by definition, the older they get the cleverer they get, and they will try many tricks to get rid of the hounds. Deer are herd animals, and when hunted they often try to run to other deer. With a stag, a trained eye can follow his progress, and see when he separates from the others. With a hind, with no antlers to distinguish her, it can be much more difficult. It is interesting to note that a herd often shows very little sympathy for the hunted stranger, and will often drive him or her out, in short order.

A hunted stag will often 'run the water'. The West Country abounds with streams and rivers and running water carries no scent, or rather it carries the scent away with it. It is not unknown for a hunted deer to run the water for several miles: This presents problems for hounds and huntsman. There will be no scent for the hounds to follow, so the huntsman will have to hold them on until they hit the spot where the run deer has come out of the stream; but the question is, upstream or down? The huntsman will only have the direction his hounds have been pointing to guide him; that and his local knowledge. However there will be no need for you to worry too much about it; sorting out that kind of problem is how people retain their posts as huntsmen: I suspect you may well be glad of a breather. Staghunting can be long, and fast, and very often hot, in autumn. A 13-mile point with the Devon and Somerset comes to mind: I remember that it was hot, and I think that it was September. I cannot remember where we met, but they took the stag right down by Watchet.

This brings us to the end of a deer hunt. As in other forms of hunting the deer is either killed, or gets away. Unlike with hare or fox, the hounds do not do the killing. The deer will eventually stand to bay, and the hounds do just that; they stand round the deer and bay it, just like your poodle does to Mr Jones's St Bernard. The deer is then shot. You will have seen various people riding with rather cumbersome looking leather cases on their saddles; inside the case is a folding shotgun. The deer is shot at close range, and killed instantaneously.

As a visitor you may be offered a slot, which is a great honour, and should be accepted as such. The acceptance should involve the transfer of nothing less than a £10 note to the huntsman. As I type this, I have before me on the desk, a paperweight made from a stag's slot; the inscription says 'D & S.S. – Sandyway – 20/4/65'. It was my first day's staghunting – an 11-mile point and a day that is graven in my memory for many reasons, all of them good. When I go back to Exmoor, I still get people who ask me if I 'mind that good hunt from Sandyway, when us took the stag near Mr Nancekivell's, and then you . . .'; but what comes next is absolutely my own affair unless I'm asked out to dinner and given lots of good port, when I may tell the whole story.

The head of the stag is not available to visitors; by custom it goes to a farmer or landowner who has had some connection with the day's sport. As for the carcass, all that good venison is not wasted. It gets taken away in a Land Rover, back to the area where the deer was found. In each area there is someone appointed to oversee the distribution of the bits and pieces, and hand them out around the district with the compliments of the master.

When the autumn staghunting finishes at the end of October, there is a break of about a fortnight – a very sensible idea. Three long, hard galloping days a week, for three months, over some of the hardest country, and sometimes in foul weather conditions, take their toll on men and animals. A break freshens everybody up.

In the middle of November comes the hindhunting. Harbouring is not necessary for this, and any adult hind is hunted. The difficulty is getting one hind away from the herd, and getting hounds settled on that one, after the herd has split up. I have never done much hindhunting, but the experts tell me that it is much more difficult than staghunting. Hinds are very canny, and old hinds are full of tricks. There are no antlers to help identify a deer, and to do so takes a lot of skill and experience. It is vital, however, if you want to catch your hind before

The Devon and Somerset Staghounds,
with huntsman Dennis Boyles, in Bagworthy Water

dark stops you, that hounds are not allowed to change onto fresh deer. Hindhunting continues until the end of February. There is then another fortnight's break, then the spring staghunting starts.

Spring staghunting is from the middle of March until the end of April and is when the young stags (3 to 5 years old) are hunted. They have all the confidence and lack of sense of all young creatures; they tend to be up and going, and to keep going. The cognoscenti reckon that because of this the great hunts tend to happen in the spring. I have already mentioned my paperweight hunt. That hunt was on a Tuesday. What has not yet been told is that I went back for another cut on the following Saturday and had a 14-mile point, taking the stag in the river below Filleigh Viaduct. I remember that day too, because it poured with rain all the time. At the end of the day, about 3.30, I got a lift back with the stag, and other sportsmen who were likewise going back for their transport. As we were all wet and cold, the conversation turned to whisky, or the lack of it, and the iniquity of licensing laws that came between respectable sportsmen and a drink. We turned to the Church for help; for in the front of the Land Rover was the sporting vicar of X. It was reasoned that no God-fearing Exmoor publican would refuse whisky to a staghunting man of the cloth; and so it proved. The reverend gent came trotting round from the back of the pub outside which we had halted, with a bottle of the best.

Staghunting is a unique experience, which you should miss no chance to enjoy.

Glossary

Antler: the horns on a stag, or buck.

Babbler: a hound that speaks without due cause, ie when there is no fox to speak to; this term can also be applied to humans. It is a capital offence for a hound.

Bay: the second point, counting from the skull, on the main stem of a stag's antler. A hunted stag will 'stand at bay' at the end of a hunt ie the deer will stand its ground, surrounded by the hounds, who bay at it. Foxhounds are sometimes said to bay at an earth.

Beam: main stem of antler.

Belling: the roar of a rutting stag.

Billet: old-fashioned term for fox droppings.

Blank: nothing; a blank day is a foxless day; to draw blank is to fail to find a fox or whatever quarry you may be seeking.

Border terrier: a type of terrier developed on the English/Scottish Borders. It has now been taken up by the showbench people with detrimental effect, though there are still some good working strains. They tend to be a bit temperamental, but their devotees swear by them.

Brocket: male red deer of 3 years old or less.

Brow: the first point on a stag's antler, ie closest to the skull.

Brush: a fox's tail.

Buck: male fallow deer.

Bullfinch: in the old days fences were cut and laid, usually every seven years. However if the fence was neglected it would become higher, thicker and hairier, every year. A bullfinch had to be jumped through, rather than over, with resulting damage to face and clothing, and with no way of knowing what jollity awaited you on the other side. It could be anything from an arm of the sea to a set of upturned harrows. The mechanical hedgetrimmer has largely put paid to these horrors. Even if you do come across a bullfinch, with a bit of luck it will be so heavily wired that you can seek a gate with a clear conscience.

Calf: young red deer.

Cap: the peaked hunting cap was once only worn by hunt officials. It is now in more general use, in the interests of safety. The Hon Sec would sometimes use his cap to collect the money from the punters, thus a cap has come to mean the amount you pay for a day ticket with a hunt.

Cast: what hounds should be allowed to do at a check; it is the action of seeking to recover the line they have been hunting.

Check: exactly what it says; a check in the hunt caused by the temporary (we hope) loss of scent, for whatever reason.

Chop: hounds chop a fox if they kill him without hunting him; perhaps he was asleep, for instance.

Clitter: northern term for a tumble of boulders on a hillside.

Coloured: when this term is applied to a horse, it indicates irregular black and white (piebald) or brown and white (shewbald) markings.

Combe: West Country name for a deep valley.

Country: a hunt's country is the area in which it has sole operational rights, as far as other hunts are concerned. The boundaries will be registered with the appropriate masters' association, and may only be changed by the mutual consent of all the hunt committees involved. The rights only apply as far as other hunts are concerned. There is no right to hunt over private land: it is a privilege dependant on the good will of the owners/occupiers. The areas registered for different types of hunting are not inter-related. The same geographical area may contain a foxhunting country, a harehunting country, and a mink hunting country: as an example, the area registered by the Devon and Somerset Staghounds for deerhunting would cover the areas registered by some five foxhound packs.

Crop: incorrect name for a hunting whip.

Cub: young fox.

Doe: female fallow deer; also female hare.

Drag: the line of a quarry that has moved some time before. In hill hunting you will often hear of hounds dragging up to their fox. It is

normally only in the hills that conditions will allow hounds to do this. Draghunting is where the hounds follow an aniseed trail over a prepared line; hunting is too dignified a term for it.

Draw: hounds draw for their quarry to find it. The area where the quarry is to be sought is the 'day's draw'.

Earth: a fox's burrow.

Feather: when a hound is working a line which he is not sure enough of to speak to, you will see his stern thrashing; this is 'feathering'.

Feument: deer's dung; a somewhat archaic term.

First whipper-in and kennel huntsman: a man with equal status to a professional huntsman, in that he is in charge of the hounds, but whips in to the master who hunts the hounds.

Foil: smells that interfere with the scent of the quarry, so you can have sheep foil, cattle foil etc. A quarry that runs back on its own line is said to 'run foil'.

Form: the resting place of a hare.

Full cry: when all hounds are speaking together.

Funerals: it is a generally accepted belief that hunted foxes run to funerals, and there does sometimes seem to be an other-worldly side to foxes. My favourite story concerns the old Earl of Harrington who hunted his own hounds, in Nottinghamshire, from 1882 to his death in 1917. The day after he was buried, hounds hunted as usual, as he had directed. The late Earl had an enormous grey beard. Strange to relate hounds found at once, in the first covert, a huge grey fox. There then followed a desperately fast hunt, in which the horses were left far behind. They found the hounds lying round the old lord's grave. The huntsman said: 'His Lordship has called his hounds: I think we should go home', and no one disagreed with him.

Goyle: West Country term for a small valley.

Guarantee: masters used to enter into a yearly contract with their hunt committees (1 May to 30 April; notice on either side by 1 February). The master undertook to hunt the country X days per week, in return for which the committee 'guaranteed' the master(s) a certain sum of money towards the exes. Any excess of expenditure over income was the master's responsibility. This open-ended commitment was found to be unacceptable to an increasing number of masters. The normal situation today is that the master has a limited financial commitment (in theory, anyway), and the committee is responsible for keeping pace with inflation.

Harbourer: in staghunting (as opposed to hindhunting), only the chosen stag is hunted. He is chosen according to his age, and fitness, relative to the time of year. It is the harbourer's job first to locate a

suitable stag, and then to discover where it is lying on the morning of the hunt; the stag is then said to be harboured.

Hike!: used by some huntsmen as a cheer to hounds; a corruption of Hark!, as in 'Hike to Smellwell!'.

Headed: a quarry is headed when it is turned from its chosen path.

Heel: hounds run heel when they run the line in the opposite direction to that taken by the quarry; also referred to as 'back line' in certain parts of the country.

Heu gaze!: otter hunting Tally-ho.

Hind: female red deer.

Holloa: pronounced holler: long drawn out screech denoting the departure of a fox from a covert.

Holt: lair of otter.

Jack: male hare.

Jack Russell: a type of terrier bred by the well-known hunting Devonshire parson of that name. Now loosely, and incorrectly, used to describe any sort of small white terrier, most of whom would have the vapours if confronted by a fox; or a vole, come to that.

Kennelman (feeder): ranks next under the huntsman in the kennel hierarchy: does not go hunting but is responsible for all the preparation of the hounds' feed, and for feeding in the huntsman's absence.

Knacker's: the carcasses of the fallen stock that are collected from the farms (thereby saving the farmer from digging a hole), and form a large part of the kennel cuisine. The knacker round thus gives a service to the farmers, and to the hunt alike. It is also a valuable method of keeping a finger on the pulse of a hunting country. Knackering is not a job for those of a sensitive nature, or weak stomach.

Lakeland: type of terrier bred in the Lake District, and surrounds. They are usually leggy and rough coated, in shades of brown and black. They are bred to be hard. Not usually suitable as pets.

Lash: the piece of whipcord on the end of the thong.

Leu in: traditional encouragement to hounds to go into a covert. Derives from the Norman *e loup* 'after the wolf', and I bet your huntsman would get a shock if he did find one.

Leveret: young hare.

Lift: a huntsman 'lifts' hounds, when he takes them off their noses and bids them accompany him to where the fox has gone, or where he thinks it has gone; not necessarily the same place at all; *see* Quick huntsmen.

Lug (ear) **mark:** all hounds have, or should have, identify tattoos in their ears. There will normally be the hunt's initials in one ear, and a litter number in the other.

Make: to count a pack of hounds; a question of practice. Hounds are numbered in couples because it is supposed to be easier to count them that way. I always count them in two couples, which is easier still; if you do not believe me, try it for yourself. Many huntsmen refuse to hunt with an even number (ie 16 or 17, couple); they always have the half couple for luck.

March: boundary.

Mark: when hounds hunt a fox into a hole, they are said to mark it.

Mask: the head of the fox.

Mort: old name for the call blown at the kill, now more commonly known as the 'rattle'; bears no relation to the fanfare that is called *mort* in France.

Mute: a hound is said to be mute when it hunts without speaking; a capital offence.

New ley (or seeds): You will sometimes see this written on a gate, or on a sign stuck in a field. It means that the field has been newly sown with grass seed (expensive and delicate), and should on no account be ridden over. You may think that this is too obvious to need stating, but I once stood by a gate with such a sign and listened to two top hatted gents speculating as to the identity of 'Mr Newley'.

Old pasture: permanent grass that has been unploughed for yonks; sometimes a hundred years or more. At one time the bulk of the farmland in Great Britain was old pasture, and this was the golden age of hunting. Most of it has now been promiscuously ripped up to add to the grain mountain. Many farmers will come to bitterly regret the passing of their old grasses.

Point: people placed strategically around a covert to watch for the departure of a fox, are said to be 'on point'. The 'point' of a hunt is the longest distance in a straight line that may occur in that hunt; for instance, a twisting fox might take hounds for 12 miles, and still never be more than 3 miles from where he was found; this would be described as 'a hunt of some 15 miles [hunt scribes are human], but no more than a 4-mile [see what I mean] point.'

Oxer: with a bit of luck you will never encounter one of these; they used to occur in grass countries, and consisted of a cut and laid hedge, with a ditch on one, or both sides, which was protected by a split oak 'ox rail'. They took a lot of jumping. The Pytchley country was particularly infamous for them, and the resident thrusters reckoned that it was impossible to jump more than twelve consecutive oxers without getting a fall. The oak rails are now replaced by wire.

Pad: foot of fox or hare.

Quick huntsmen: come in two categories. First, men capable of

thinking quickly and acting upon the thought – a virtue; second, men who interpret quickness as never leaving their hounds alone and who are always lifting them about the countryside. This loses foxes, quickly, and ruins hounds equally quickly; hopefully exit huntsman, quickly.

Rape: We are talking about oil seed rape. I know of no recorded instance of the other variety in the hunting field although, now I come to think of it, there was the case of Squire 'Mad Jack' Mytton. He was hacking on to the meet, one day, when he met a girl carrying a basket of eggs to market. He stripped her; tied her to a gate post, raped her, and then pelted her with her eggs. You may be relieved to hear that he died, drunk, broke and consumptive, in Boulogne. Oil seed rape is another of the stretches of green that you will encounter in the winter countryside. It is an expensive and sensitive crop, and does not benefit from being ridden over.

Rattle *see* Mort.

Ride: a way cut through a wood.

Rights: to do with the antlers of the red-deer stag; he has his rights when he has his full complement of points on the antler – brow, bay, trey and three on top.

Riot: usually mainly in foxhunting; hounds riot when they hunt anything except the fox. If beagles were to hunt a fox, I suppose that that would also be riot.

Royal: a stag with twelve, or more, antler points. I think that this term is only used in Scotland.

Rut: Mating season for red, and fallow, deer; October to November.

Scut: hare's tail.

Seal: otter's footprints.

See ho!: harehunting equivalent of Tally-ho!

Skirter: a hound that cuts corners, or goes round the edge of a covert instead of going into the nasty prickles; such hounds are not kept.

Slack: a northern goyle, ie small valley.

Slot: footprint of deer, or the foot itself.

Soil: hunted deer sometimes take to water, and often stand at bay in it; they are then said to have 'taken soil'.

Spraint: otter's droppings.

Stern: hound's tail.

Stop: a fox's earth is 'stopped' to prevent it going to ground during a hunt. It is usually done by shovelling earth into the holes, and should be done after closing time, when the fox is likely to be out on its rounds. In an ideal situation the earth should be checked in the morning to see if the fox has dug itself back in again. In practice holes tend

to get blocked in the morning, before hunting. This practice is known as 'putting to', and very often results in the fox being blocked in for the day.

Stub-bred fox: one that has been born above ground.

Stud groom: senior groom in charge of the stables; usually men, and ladies, of formidable personality.

Stuggy: literally 'sticky'; West Country word for boggy ground.

Subscription: the fee you pay to become a member of a hunt.

Syke: northern goyle, ie small valley.

Tally ho!: we all know that that is what we say when we see a fox; but do we know why? It derives from Norman French *il est haut* 'he is raised'. Try saying it fast, several times in succession, and the light will dawn upon you.

Thong: the plaited leather whippy part of a hunting whip.

Trey: the third antler point.

Tufter *see* Chapter 11.

Velvet: stags shed their antlers in the spring. The new growth is soft, and vulnerable. The new horn hardens gradually, and has a covering which is eventually rubbed off: this is the 'velvet'.

Vent: when an otter comes to the surface to breathe.

Vixen: bitch fox.

Warrantable: a huntable stag. Old stags of 5 years plus are hunted in autumn (August, September, October). The young stags (3–5 years) are hunted in spring.

Whelp: hound puppy.

Whins: northern word for gorse.

Whip: incorrectly called a crop: should always have a thong and a lash. Should never be used as an abbreviation for whipper-in.

Whipper-in: huntsman's assistant.

Who whoop!: an approximation of the noise made by the huntsman at the kill.

Winter corn: corn planted in autumn that germinates through the winter, and looks green and inviting. In fact it is not harmed by being galloped over, but many farmers think that it is, which comes to the same thing. Go round the edge.

Further Reading

Most of the books recommended here are out of print. Your local secondhand book shop may not be very helpful. As this is a rather specialised area you will do better to consult specialists. Sporting book experts advertise in magazines such as *Horse and Hound,* and *Hounds.* J. A. Allen & Co, 1 Lower Grosvenor Place, Buckingham Palace Road, London, SW1W 0EL, have long been leaders in this field.

Baily's Hunting Directory (J. A. Allen): published annually; gives details of all known hunts throughout the world. You may not wish to buy a copy every year, but you should certainly have an occasional copy.

Beckford, Peter. *Thoughts on Hunting:* one of the three great textbooks on hunting; a must.

Bell, Isaac. *Huntsman's Log Book; Foxiana;* and any other titles: 'Ikey' Bell was an American, who became one of the most famous masters of his generation. He was one of the leading 'Young Turks' who helped to develop the 'modern' foxhound. He was a highly entertaining writer.

Broke, Lord Willoughby de. *Hunting the Fox:* to my mind the best hunting textbook written this century. It will give you a good insight into what your huntsman is, or should be, doing. I used to reread it

every year when I was hunting hounds, and followed His Lordship's precepts with what, in all modesty, I can say was some degree of success.

Buchanan-Jardine, Sir John. *Hounds of the World:* will tell you all you want to know about all types of hound.

Budgett, H. M. *Hunting by Scent:* this is supposed to be the definitive book on scent. I have never yet been able to land a copy.

Clapham, Richard. *The Book of the Fox*, and any other titles: a great authority on fell hunting.

Moore, Daphne. Any titles: Miss Moore is a great authority on hounds and hunting, and is very readable.

Smith, Thomas. *Diary of a Huntsman:* the third great textbook on hunting the fox.

Somerville & Ross. *Some Experiences of an Irish R.M.; Further Experiences of an Irish R.M.; In Mr Knox's Country;* and any other titles: do not be put off by the disgraceful television production of these lovely stories. Try to get editions with the original illustrations. I hope that you will reread them as often as I do.

Stanford, J. K. *Death of Vulpecide*, and any other titles: amusing books.

Surtees, R. S. All titles: start with *Handley Cross;* then luxuriate in the rest; truly wonderful stuff.

Magazines: *Horse and Hound; Hounds* (subscription only), Rose Cottage, Hughley, Shrewsbury, Shropshire SY5 6HX.) Both required reading.

Index